The Amazins

CELEBRATING 50 YEARS
OF NEW YORK METS HISTORY

TRIUMPH
BOOKS

(AP Images)

No part of this publication may be reproduced, stored in a retrieval system, or transmitted in any form by any means, electronic, mechanical, photocopying, or otherwise, without the prior written permission of the publisher, Triumph Books, 542 South Dearborn Street, Suite 750, Chicago, Illinois 60605.

Triumph Books and colophon are registered trademarks of Random House, Inc.

This book is available in quantity at special discounts for your group or organization. For further information, contact:

Triumph Books
542 South Dearborn Street
Suite 750
Chicago, Illinois 60605
(312) 939-3330
Fax (312) 663-3557
www.triumphbooks.com

Printed in China
ISBN: 978-1-60078-611-2
Design by Dustin Hubbart

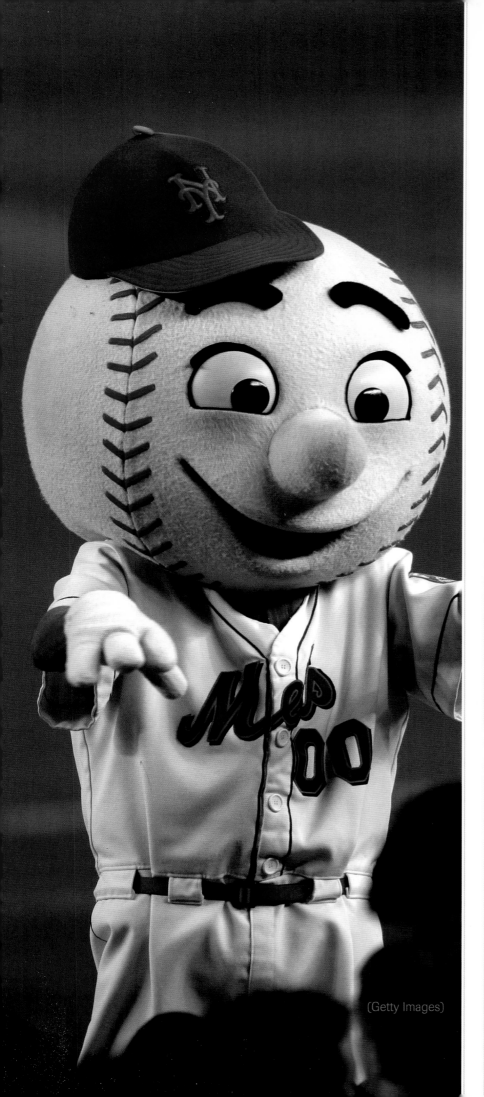

(Getty Images)

Contents

INDUCTED: 1981

INDUCTED: 1981

CHARLES DILLON "CASEY" STENGEL
MANAGER 1962-1965
VICE PRESIDENT 1965-1975

NEW YORK BASEBALL INSTITUTION AND SEVEN-TIME
WORLD SERIES WINNING MANAGER WAS LURED OUT OF
RETIREMENT TO BECOME THE METS FIRST
MANAGER...FANS GREW TO LOVE THE METS AS STENGEL'S
CHARISMATIC PERSONALITY AND WITTY OBSERVATIONS
OFFSET THE CLUB'S STRUGGLES IN ITS INFANCY... HIS 37
WAS THE FIRST METS NUMBER TO BE RETIRED
(1965)...ELECTED TO THE NATIONAL BASEBALL HALL OF
FAME IN 1966.

INDUCTED: 1981

GEORGE M. WEISS
PRESIDENT 1962-1966

THE METS FIRST PRESIDENT WHO LAID THE FOUNDATION
FOR THE 1969 WORLD SERIES CHAMPIONSHIP TEAM...HIRED
CASEY STENGEL TO BECOME THE METS FIRST
MANAGER...UNDER HIS LEADERSHIP THE METS FOUND
AND DEVELOPED TOM SEAVER, NOLAN RYAN AND TUG
McGRAW...WON SEVEN WORLD SERIES CHAMPIONSHIPS AS
A GENERAL MANAGER BEFORE JOINING THE METS...ELECTED
TO THE NATIONAL BASEBALL HALL OF FAME IN 1971.

INDUCTED: 1989

A Mets fan views plaques at the New York Mets Hall of Fame and Museum at Citi Field. (AP Images)

Introduction

By Mike Vaccaro

Question: How many sports franchises do you know that double as forever metaphors?

Okay: There are the '27 Yankees, the '72 Dolphins, and the '96 Bulls, all dominant teams in their respective sports; whenever a team is playing especially well, you hear lots of talk that goes this way: "Well, they're good, but they're not exactly the '27 Yankees yet." Or, "Well, the Heat looks terrific, but they're a long way from the '96 Bulls."

Here's another question: how many sports franchises do you know that can serve as two entirely separate forever metaphors, representing two entirely different places on the sporting spectrum?

The answer to that is much simpler: only one.

Only the New York Mets.

Think about it. If you're managing a Little League team, or playing on a softball team, or even on an historic run of bad beats in your neighborhood poker game, as likely as not you or someone you know is going to make an instant comparison.

That team is the '62 Mets of our league…

And everyone—everyone—will know exactly what that means.

But there's this too: in those wonderful moments when sports surprises us, when it gives us the kind of out-of-the-clear-blue-sky bombshell that sports can truly specialize in, there's another comparison. And it's the best one of all. Think of all the remarkable upsets that have happened over the past few decades: the U.S. 1980 Olympic hockey team, the '83 N.C. State and '85 Villanova basketball teams, the 2008 Giants knocking off the undefeated Patriots. All of them, at one time or another, were likened to a singular time and a singular team.

Still don't believe? Heck, God Himself (disguised as George Burns) once put it this way: "My last miracle was the '69 Mets."

So this is the team we celebrate and commemorate in these pages, a baseball team conceived in the vacuum left behind by the treacherous exiles of the New York Giants and Brooklyn Dodgers, one that was born in the shadow of their imperial neighbors, the Yankees, and raised in the '60s, a time of turbulence when it felt the world was turning upside down—and when the Mets, in the decade's last year, proved it. A team that nearly vanished from irrelevance in the '70s, that rose once again in the '80s to become the sport's dominant brand. And has continued to today to carry on a deep, proud National League legacy in a city, New York, that has forever considered itself a National League town, despite all the championship hardware collected by the American League team.

No, the Mets—and the people who care about them, root for them, sustain them, live with them and die with them—are every bit as meaningful a part of the baseball fabric as any of their ancestors and any of their peers. They captured the city's imagination even as they lost 120 games in their first year, even as they lost 737 games in their first seven years of existence, a stretch of unabashed futility unmatched anywhere in baseball history.

In those early years, even with the losses they managed to close the business gap between themselves and the Yankees, siphoning off fans and drawing customers to old Shea Stadium in numbers that belied logic. In 1964, the last year of the classic Yankees dynasty, the Yanks won 99 games and made it to Game 7 of the World Series; the Mets lost 109 games and finished 40 games out of first place.

The Yankees drew 1.3 million fans, the Mets close to 1.75 million.

Later, when the Mets started to acquire and develop better players, that devotion only swelled: Tom Seaver and Cleon Jones became the team's first home-grown stars. Jerry Koosman and Jerry Grote, Bud Harrelson and Wayne Garrett became the core for the 1969 champions and the 1973 National League pennant winners that came within a skinny game of a second title. Old-time New York heroes Gil Hodges and Yogi Berra were high-profile managers who oversaw this rise; at one point in '69, Mets games on local television averaged a 50 share among all people with a TV set.

They were bombarded in nicknames: The New Breed. The Miracle Mets. The Amazin' Mets.

And later, simply, the Amazins.

It is a testament to how deep these devotions truly lie that after nearly a full decade of losing and irrelevance—during which time the Yankees re-emerged, won two World Series, and generally began to outdraw the Mets 2-to-1—that the Mets were able to recapture the town almost completely by 1986, collecting a cavalcade of stars such as Keith Hernandez, Gary Carter, Dwight Gooden, and Darryl Strawberry—to name four—that romped to 108 wins and won the franchise's second title thanks to gut-churning survival tests against the Astros and Red Sox in the playoffs.

(You want another forever-sports metaphor, by the way? Gather a room full of Mets fans and Sox fans. Ask them what the words "Game 6" mean to them. And then get out of the way.)

The years since '86 have been alternately unkind and sublime for the team, a testament to the fact that the Mets have never been the huge-market metronome that the Yankees are. But there have been moments aplenty. There was a one-game playoff in 1999, in which Al Leiter—who grew up a Mets fan—pitched them into their first postseason in 11 years by throwing a two-hitter at the Reds. A few weeks later, Robin Ventura would invent a new way to win a playoff game: the "walk-off grand single." In 2000, the Mets costarred in the first Subway Series in 44 years, a joyous event that gripped New York City in a way few sporting extravaganzas ever have. Six years later, Endy Chavez would stop the city's collective heart with a breathtaking catch in Game 7 of the NL Championship Series, even if the Mets would break that heart a few innings later.

Fifty years, 50,000 memories. And counting. That is who the Mets have been from day one, and who they remain. In a city that never sleeps, they provide one more reason for a wonderful bout of insomnia.

Two of the best pitchers of their respective eras, Tom Seaver (left) and Dwight Gooden, pose together at Shea Stadium in 1987. (AP Images)

Stars of the 1960s, '70s, and '80s

Former Mets (from left) Dwight Gooden, Tom Seaver, Darryl Strawberry, and Yogi Berra participate in the "Shea Goodbye" festivities prior to the last game at Shea Stadium on September 28, 2008. (Charles Wenzelberg/New York Post)

Marv Throneberry

Born: September 2, 1933 **Died:** June 23, 1994
Height: 6'1" **Weight:** 190 lbs
Bats: Left **Throws:** Left

	Games	Ave	Hits	HR	RBI	SB
Mets (1962-63)	130	.240	89	16	50	1
Career (1955-63)	480	.237	281	53	170	3

Throneberry Has a Bad Day
First Baseman's Legendary Gaffes Symbolize Expansion Mets' Futility

June 18, 1962
By Leonard Koppett

Marvin Eugene Throneberry is a born Met—that is, his initials are M.E.T. He is also the most unusual Met—one who is thoroughly unpopular with the small but noisy and otherwise fanatically loyal group of Met fans.

No one, of course, pretends that the Mets are going to "do well." By no standard can their following be called large, despite the special case of the recent Polo Grounds crowds and yelling that so tirelessly have drenched the area with love. Encouragement and appreciation greet the slightest Met achievement—a putout, a walk, a pitcher lasting more than two innings, a loud foul. The actual scoring of a run is cause for open rejoicing, and any effort, however futile it turns out to be, brings forth applause.

But not for Marv. For some reason, he's an automatic focus for audible dissatisfaction. That is, he gets booed to bits whenever he appears.

And yesterday he had a bad, bad day.

He knew he was going to play right through a double-header, because Gil Hodges, after playing Friday night and Saturday afternoon, had a puffed-up knee again. It was hot, the team was in a losing streak, and there were about 13,000 customers on hand in no mood to make excuses because the opposition now was the Cubs.

In the top half of the first inning of the first game, the first Cub batter walked and the second struck out. As he fanned, the runner, Don Landrum, was caught between first and second. In the run-down, Landrum bumped into Throneberry, the umpire ruled interference by Marv, and a sure out was nullified as Landrum was awarded second base.

The next batter bounced out, which would have retired the side. But then came a walk, a triple, and a homer and Chicago had a 4-0 lead—on four unearned runs stemming from Throneberry's interference.

In the bottom half of the inning, the Mets had one run back, two men on, and one out when Marv came to bat. He drove the ball deep to right center, between the fielders, scoring two runs, and steamed into third. For a moment, he seemed vindicated.

But only for a moment. Suddenly, the pitcher had a new ball, and was tossing it to first base. The umpire was waving, and Throneberry was walking, red-faced, back to the dugout.

He had failed to touch first base.

The runs counted, because the appeal play made only the second out. (If there had been two out when he hit the ball, the runs would have been nullified too). As it was, Marv lost his hit, was charged with a time at bat, but did get credit for two runs batted in. But when Charley Neal hit the next pitch against the roof, the Mets were deprived of the run they would have had if Throneberry had still been on base.

So with 17 innings still to play, Marv had pulled two unusual, painfully public rocks that cost his team a total of five runs.

You can imagine the sounds that greeted him the rest of the day. And as things turned out, he had repeated opportunities for belated heroism. In the ninth inning of the opener, with Chicago now leading 8-7 and the tying run on first, he fanned, ending the game. In the second game, after booting a grounder by the first man up, he did knock in a run with a bases-loaded fly. But he struck out with two on and two out in the fifth, when Cub pitcher Bob Buhl was trailing 3-1 and was on the ropes. The Mets never scored again and lost, 4-3.

It had to be the most miserable day of his baseball life.

"Why do you say it has to be?" said Marv calmly, a half hour after it was over. "They boo me all the time. It wasn't that much worse today!"

Why do they?

"I think it's because they want to see Hodges play instead of me," said Marv. "But I try not to let it bother me. Of course, you can't really shut it out; you hear it, and it makes you mad. But I'm sort of used to it. I've been booed plenty in my time, and the fans here always have to have some target. Maybe it's better that they choose me than someone else who may be bothered more by it."

Marv Throneberry, the Mets' first baseman in 1962, looks on after being acquired from Baltimore in May 1962. Throneberry contributed 16 home runs and 49 RBIs to the first Mets team, but was often booed by Mets fans. (AP Images)

Why has he always been booed?

"Well, in the minors, I always had good years, and the fans in the other cities would give me a good going over. That's natural. In the majors, I never got a chance to play regularly, and I never hit the way people expected, I guess. I think they expect too much from me. They don't realize that I haven't really played for four years, and you simply can't hit coming off the bench. At least I can't."

Throneberry's big years were 1956 and 1957 at Denver as he led the American Assn. in homers and runs batted in. In the next two seasons with the Yankees, he got to bat 150 times one year and 192 the next. At Kansas City in 1960, he batted 236 times, and moving from the A's to the Orioles during last season, 226. His lifetime totals, going into this season, were 37 homers, 120 runs batted in, and a .238 average for the equivalent of less than two full seasons (806 at-bats).

That's not exactly no chance—but it is irregularity, and the signs of power are there.

"Well," said Marv, noting that it was now 10:15 PM, "I guess I'd better go sign some autographs. Dave, see if my public is lined up out there waiting for me."

Pitcher Dave Hillman, already dressed and impatient, snorted.

"I hope they have sense enough," he said, "to have gone home."

Tom Seaver

Born: November 17, 1944
Height: 6'1"   **Weight:** 195 lbs
Bats: Right   **Throws:** Right

	W-L	ERA	IP	Hits	BB	K	CG
Mets (1967-77, 1983)	198-124	2.57	3,045.2	2,431	847	2,541	171
Career (1967-1986)	311-205	2.86	4,783.0	3,971	1,390	3,640	231

Seaver Savors Memories Tom Terrific Bows Out

June 23, 1987
By Maury Allen

He burst upon the scene at Shea 20 years ago with boyish enthusiasm in the clubhouse and grizzled determination on the mound. He left yesterday in complete control of his last press conference, utterly confident he was doing the right thing.

The choir-boy good looks were still there, and so were the self-deprecating wit, the absolute control of his own destiny.

Yet he quit because he wasn't Tom Seaver anymore.

More than half an hour into the press conference, with the questions running down, he was asked about the toughest hitters he had faced. The answer was supposed to be Johnny Bench or Willie McCovey or Willie Stargell.

"Barry Lyons was very tough," he said. Then he exploded in that Seaver cackle, the laughter coming from his shoe tops and lighting up the room.

Seaver had allowed Lyons to hit a pitch into the bullpen in a simulated game last Saturday. It was the final message.

"I went to the bench each inning and thought about what I had done," he said. "I took those pitches to the bench, and I thought about Mike Schmidt and Tim Raines, and I realized I was in trouble."

He appeared, as he had in most of his big moments, with Nancy Seaver at his side. She looked lovely in a light blue suit, her hair the golden glow first seen at Shea 20 years ago in those seats behind home plate. The Seavers were holding hands when they entered the old Jets' locker room. Dressed in a dark jacket and white slacks, Seaver looked exactly like what he was: a retired businessman about to go on vacation.

He talked lightly of the past. "I've had a beautiful run, so many lovely things have happened to me," he said. "I leave with a deep sense of contentment."

We all thought back a couple of decades. Nancy remembered the first time she saw him pitch a professional game, in Jacksonville.

"It was 21 years ago, just after our wedding in June. I was sitting in the stands with the wife of pitcher Darrell Sutherland. I had grown up in Kansas and moved to California. All my family were Yankee fans, Mickey Mantle fans, but I didn't know anything about baseball. Then she said Tom was in the batter's circle. I said, 'Where's the batter's circle?'"

They were an entry when they came to Shea, she in those orange tam-o'-shanter hats, he, The Franchise—Rookie of the Year in 1967, a 16-game winner in 1968, the leader and Cy Young winner in 1969.

"He was the player who had the single greatest impact on this franchise," Frank Cashen said yesterday.

Seaver said his 300th win with the White Sox at Yankee Stadium in 1985 and the 1969 world championship, with teammates like Buddy Harrelson and a manager like Gil Hodges, were his fondest memories.

I have another. It pinpointed the kind of player Seaver really was. It was 1969. The Mets had won a game in Atlanta that put them at .500 for the first time in their history. The joy in the clubhouse at this miraculous event was bountiful. Seaver scowled when we reporters asked him to comment on the occasion.

"We haven't done anything yet," he said.

This was a man who would not settle for second best. The jokes about Marvelous Marv Throneberry and Casey Stengel were not part of his history. No one would laugh at a champion.

There were some jealousies in those days, about the Tom and Nancy thing, about the nicknames Tom Terrific and The Franchise, about the identification of this team revolving around one pitcher. He had his friends on those teams. He had his detractors. Nobody denied his skills.

Like Babe Ruth, Lou Gehrig, Joe DiMaggio, Stan Musial, Ted Williams, and Bob Feller, Seaver's identification with his team was emotional. The bond was broken over an ugly contract hassle in 1977, when he forced a trade after he couldn't force a contract extension.

There were enough angry words on all sides to last a lifetime. Seaver wouldn't touch any of that yesterday as he said his calm farewells. He wouldn't talk of the hurts of 1977 or the

Tom Seaver holds the Mets franchise records for wins, earned run average, innings pitched, complete games, and shutouts. (Getty Images)

disappointment of his second farewell address in 1984.

His only show of unpleasantness occurred when he was forced to remind a television reporter that only one person at a time talked at a Seaver press conference, and when Seaver was at the microphone it was not to be a television voice.

He joked about his future. "I was offered the ABC news job at six," he said, "but I turned it down. I would have to have a divorce or lose my right arm."

He would go home now to be with Nancy and his two daughters, to enjoy a year off before starting a new phase of his life, to sit quietly in that big old converted barn in Greenwich and savor 311 victories.

There was one more Seaver moment. Somebody mentioned the name of Jimmy Qualls, the trivia Cub who broke up his 1969 perfect game.

"Why don't you go suck a lemon?" Seaver said.

Then came Rusty Staub and Harrelson with a gift of wine.

"I'll save the bottle, I'll save the memories," he said, "but I won't save the wine."

Right: Tom Seaver pitches at Shea Stadium during the 1969 season. Seaver won a league-high 25 games for the World Series champions. (Getty Images)

Below: Tom Seaver plants a kiss on Tom Glavine after Glavine won his 300th game in August 2007. Glavine joined Seaver, who finished with 311 career victories, in the exclusive club of 300-game winners. (Getty Images)

Jerry Koosman

Born: December 23, 1942
Height: 6'2" **Weight:** 205 lbs
Bats: Right **Throws:** Left

	W-L	ERA	IP	Hits	BB	K	CG
Mets (1967-78)	140-137	3.09	2,544.2	2,281	820	1,799	108
Career (1967-85)	222-209	3.36	3,839.1	3,635	1,198	2,556	140

Wasting No Time Few Idle Moments in Pitcher's Career

April 14, 1986
By Pete Coutros

Spring will be a little late in Minnesota this year, but Jerry Koosman is willing to wait.

"This is the first time in 21 years that I'm out of baseball, the first time in all those years that I haven't gone south for training camp, so it's been a long time since I've seen the grass turn green or watched new leaves sprouting on trees," says Koosman, turning up the thermostat half a notch.

At 43, Kooz is home in Chaska, a southern suburb of Minneapolis, where spring is perennially laggard.

"I haven't picked up a ball yet this year," said Jerry, who last spring was oiling up his trusty arm for one more season in the sun.

"Being home this year means I'll be able to go to the confirmation of my daughter, Danielle, and it means I'll be there when my son, Shawn, graduates from high school," said Koosman, pleased at the prospect of spending quality time with his family—including his wife and his eldest son, Mike, 18—after all those years on the road.

Does he miss any of it? "I miss some of the guys. I talked with Steve Carlton over the winter, but I can't say I miss the training routine," he said. Nor is he avidly pursuing the exploits of former teammates in the sports pages.

"Once in a while I take a look at what's happening down there, but most of the time I'm too busy with other things. Right now I'm in the process of getting an international courier business off the ground."

The name of the company is Air Systems, Inc. It is based in Long Island City, and if its delivery is half as fast as Koosman's used to be, it should go places in a hurry.

He never wasted much time. In his first full year at Shea in 1968 he won 18 games and lost a photo finish for Rookie

of the Year honors to Reds catcher Johnny Bench. Koosman threw seven shutouts that year, matching the record for whitewashes by a freshman.

For good reason, one of those calcimine jobs is more indelibly inscribed in his mind than all the rest.

"It was our home opener at Shea, a lot of people looking at me," Jerry recalls. "We were playing the Giants, and in those days, the Giants had some power in their lineup. Guys like Mays and McCovey and Jim Ray Hart, guys who lost a lot of baseballs in the seats."

Having already pitched a shutout in Los Angeles before coming east for the debut at home, Koosman approached his assignment with some confidence. Still, it was his first season in the Mets' starting rotation, he was 24 years old, and there were all those people in the stands hoping for big things, if not dreaming of the miracle that was still a year away.

"Before I could even break a sweat, the bases were loaded, Willie Mays was at bat—and this was only the first inning," Kooz remembers.

"There was a hit, an error, and then I walked somebody and, just like that, Mays was up and Jerry Grote came out to talk to me. I don't remember what he told me, but I remember asking myself what I was doing out there."

The only alternative would have been toiling on his father's 400-acre farm in Appleton, Minn., so Koosman only considered that option briefly. He reached down for the resin bag, squeezed it twice, dropped it behind the rubber, and stared at Grote for the sign, knowing all the time exactly what he would be serving to Mays.

"Willie was a guess hitter, and somewhere along the way, I picked up on some of his mannerisms which clued me in on what he was looking for," Jerry said. "When Willie was looking fastball he moved his left foot closer to the plate. If he was anticipating a curve, he would open up his stance."

As Mays confronted Koosman, Say Hey's left foot edged perceptibly closer to the plate.

"I knew what he was looking for and he probably knew that I knew, but I decided to go with my best stuff, so I threw him nothing but fastballs. I finally struck him out swinging. I stayed with the heat and popped Hart to Grote and then I got Hiatt for the third out. That was the roughest inning I had in the whole game and I wound up winning on a shutout, 3-0."

Hiatt? Ah, that would be Jack Hiatt, journeyman catcher, a name widely forgotten—but not by Koosman. "You never forget a name like that one, never."

Jerry Koosman pitches against the Athletics during
Game 2 of the 1973 World Series. (Getty Images)

Bud Harrelson

Born: June 6, 1944
Height: 5'11" **Weight:** 150 lbs
Bats: Both **Throws:** Right

	Games	Ave	Hits	HR	RBI	SB
Mets (1965–77)	1,322	.234	1,029	6	242	115
Career (1965–80)	1,533	.236	1,120	7	267	127

Big Asset All-Star Shortstop Makes the Most of His 150 Pounds

July 30, 1970
By Maury Allen

Jerry Grote, conked on the head by Mike Jorgensen's batting practice home run, was carried into the Mets clubhouse yesterday afternoon feet first on a stretcher.

"If they want me," said Bud Harrelson, "I'll catch."

Grote survived the blow to his hard head but the picture of Harrelson, disappearing under the mask, chest protector, and shin guards, was too awful to contemplate. Could a mouse stand up and proclaim himself king of the jungle?

It all sounds ludicrous until one examines the tough hide and competitiveness in the Mets' 150-going-on-140-pound All-Star shortstop. It isn't surprising that Harrelson could go behind the bat in an emergency. It's a miracle he is here at all.

Major league ball clubs aren't filled with sunken-cheeked 150-pounders who play the most grueling position on the field through the dog days of summer.

"I always lose weight during the season," said Harrelson. "I can't eat much after a game. If I'm not playing in a game I go into the clubhouse afterwards and eat everything in sight."

Harrelson has been playing the kind of shortstop envisioned for him when he walked into the Mets' Instructional League camp in 1964. He is hitting with great skills and only missed by four bases of hitting for the cycle the other night. Gil Hodges deprived him of his chance by resting him.

"He didn't want me to hit that home run," said Harrelson. "It would cause the writers too much trouble."

The home run would not be all that unexpected. Harrelson hits a home run every four years whether he wants to or not.

"I guess I've heard more about his first one than any home run ever hit by a Met," said Hodges.

On Aug. 17, 1967, Harrelson dropped a fly ball into the right-field corner in Pittsburgh's Forbes Field. While Al Luplow decided it was foul as it came to rest in the nearby open bullpen, the umpire decided it was fair.

"The guys in the bullpen grabbed Luplow, turned him around, and told him to get his butt back out there again," said Harrelson.

Before all that was said and done Harrelson was across home plate.

On April 17 of this very year he right-handed a line drive into the Phillies' bullpen against left-hander Grant Jackson.

"I don't go for home runs," Harrelson confessed. "I learned that you do what you can do."

Whitey Herzog took Harrelson five years ago and helped make him a switch hitter. It made him an All-Star.

"I was anxious to learn," he said. "I knew I could get to play every day. Don Kessinger was already doing it in the major leagues and Maury Wills had done it in the minors. It wasn't that unusual."

Harrelson has proved again that there is definitely a place for 150-pounders in the game. All they need is talent.

"I think all teams would like more giants but scouts don't disregard anybody because of size anymore. I think the success of so many small men like Phil Rizzuto and Wills and Kessinger and myself has changed that."

The small shortstop has had some pretty good days at Shea but his best was last Saturday. That's when Timothy Harrelson, age one, and a 30-pound brute, made his debut.

"He was only the star of the game," said Harrelson of the Family Day performance of his big son. "We bunted and I carried him to first. Then he jumped on the bag. We walked to second and he did a hook slide right in. We got to third and he sat down and played with the dirt. We headed home and he started to go the other way. I finally had to pick him up and carry him across. He had a good time. He never cried once. That kind of thing can be pretty frightening for a little kid."

So can playing shortstop for the world champions. But this little kid has done it splendidly: Who says he couldn't block home plate on a sliding 200-pound, spikes-high truck horse?

Mets shortstop Bud Harrelson throws the ball to first base during a 1969 game against the Pittsburgh Pirates. Harrelson was named to the All-Star team in both 1970 and 1971. (Getty Images)

Tug McGraw

Born: August 30, 1944 **Died:** January 5, 2004
Height: 6'0" **Weight:** 170 lbs
Bats: Right **Throws:** Left

A New Ballgame for McGraw
Stopper Closes Out Stellar Career

	W–L	ERA	IP	Hits	BB	K	SV
Mets (1965–74)	47–55	3.17	792.2	685	350	618	86
Career (1965–84)	96–92	3.14	1,514.2	1,318	582	1,109	180

February 16, 1985
By Maury Allen

"This is like being traded from the Mets to the Phillies," said Tug McGraw. "I am only changing lanes in my life."

McGraw announced his retirement as a pitcher the other day, but is on the threshold of an exciting after-baseball life, possibly in the office of commissioner Peter Ueberroth, maybe with the Phillies in marketing, and certainly in his own Tug McGraw Resource Company.

"When I was traded to the Phillies [10 years ago], things happened so fast and turned out so well I never had any chance to regret it," the 40-year-old left-hander said yesterday.

McGraw begins the second phase of his playing career next week, when he plays right field for the Bailey's Copy Center team in the Delaware Valley Softball League.

"They wanted me to pitch," he said. "I told them I was a hitter, not a pitcher. I'll be out there slamming the ball."

McGraw, born in Joe DiMaggio's hometown of Martinez, Cal., joined the Met organization out of high school in 1964. He made the Mets as a 20-year-old with an impressive screwball in 1965, a favorite of manager Casey Stengel and pitching coach Warren Spahn, both of whom admired his guts and his guile.

McGraw was a nervous starter then and it was Gil Hodges who told McGraw in 1969, "You can stay here as a relief pitcher or go back to the minors and work as a starter." He chose to stay.

McGraw's retirement, incidentally, marks the career end of the last player to play for Stengel.

McGraw was 9–3 on the Miracle Mets of 1969 and had 25 saves for the 1973 Met pennant-winners. He also changed the face of Met baseball forever with his rallying cry, "Ya gotta believe."

Board chairman M. Donald Grant had addressed the Mets when they were seemingly out of the race and when he left the clubhouse, McGraw yelled, "Ya gotta believe." Grant first thought he was being mocked, but as the slogan caught on and the Mets, under Yogi Berra, stole the pennant, Grant and McGraw shared that joyous triumph.

In 1975 he had a growth removed from his back. The Mets were concerned about him and sent him off to Philadelphia. Many people believed the Mets had shipped away damaged goods as McGraw soon underwent corrective surgery. The trade was the beginning of 10 years of depressing Met baseball.

"I have to thank Gil and Johnny Murphy for my career," McGraw said. "They were the most influential and then later Dallas Green [Phils manager and GM]. I had great times in New York and Philadelphia."

McGraw cited his first game ever in the big leagues at Candlestick Park with his dad in the stands as his greatest thrill. "That and beating Sandy Koufax were the two biggest games," he said. "I took pride in the World Series teams I played on and the roll I was on as a pitcher in the second half of 1973 and again in 1980 [when he helped the Phils win the World Series]."

McGraw said Tim Foli, Rennie Stennett, Pete Rose, and Roberto Clemente were his toughest hitters to get out, with all others being tied for fifth.

"Now, instead of 50,000 people cheering me on, I'll have my wife and two kids cheering me on every day," he said. "My favorite words used to be, 'Get McGraw up.' Now it will be, 'Daddy, get up.' When I decided to quit last week I bought a pair of skis. We'll all be going skiing. It will be my first time in 21 years."

The lovable left-hander said he felt honored to be considered for a job with the commissioner. He has already checked the commuting schedule from his Philadelphia home.

"I haven't ended my baseball life. I've just moved it into another phase," he said.

Baseball has to take advantage of this goodwill ambassador for the game. Ya gotta believe he can do it some good.

Tug McGraw saved 86 games for the Mets over nine seasons. The closer coined the slogan "Ya gotta believe" in 1973 when the Mets overcame a large deficit to win the National League pennant. (Getty Images)

Tommie Agee

Born: August 9, 1942   **Died:** January 22, 2001
Height: 5'11"   **Weight:** 195 lbs
Bats: Right   **Throws:** Right

	Games	Ave	Hits	HR	RBI	SB
Mets (1968-72)	661	.262	632	82	433	92
Career (1962-73)	1,129	.255	999	130	265	167

'69 Was A Blast
Outfielder's Blast Reached Shea's Upper Deck

July 15, 1994
By Ray McNulty

It went up like a flare, high into the cool spring-afternoon sky above Shea Stadium. It was perhaps the first sign that 1969 would be something special for the Mets.

The season was not even a week old. The expansion Expos were in town. And Tommie Agee was trying hard to forget 1968, when his .217 batting average and 17 RBIs left him wondering about his future.

"I had such a horrible year in '68," Agee recalled last night. "I knew if I didn't turn it around, I'd probably be out of baseball."

So on April 10, 1969, facing Expo left-hander Larry Jaster, Agee turned on a fastball and launched his comeback—not to mention what is still the only home run ever hit into Shea Stadium's upper deck.

To this day, no one is sure exactly where the ball landed, only that it hit one of the 60 seats in the lower section of the upper deck that hangs just inside the left-field foul pole. But that won't prevent the Mets from commemorating Agee's mammoth blast in a ceremony between games of tonight's double-header, when a plaque will be placed in the section where the ball landed.

"I guess I didn't stay around long enough to get into the Mets Hall of Fame, but at least now there will be something there to show I contributed something to the Mets," said Agee, 51, who still lives in East Elmhurst and works selling title insurance. "I'm very pleased they're doing it."

The ceremony kicks off a weekend of tributes and other festivities honoring the 1969 World Series champions. All fans attending tomorrow night's game will receive a replica of the 1969 Mets yearbook. And prior to Sunday's game, members of the '69 Mets will play a five-inning exhibition against players from other '69 teams.

That squad, which will be managed by Earl Weaver, will include Hall of Famers Ernie Banks and Juan Marichal as well as Glenn Beckert, Don Kessinger, Paul Blair, Curt Flood, Rico Carty, Rick Wise, Ellie Rodriguez, former Met Felix Millan, and Randy Hundley, father of current Met catcher Todd Hundley.

Among those expected to play for the '69 Mets are: Jerry Koosman, Cleon Jones, Ed Kranepool, Donn Clendenon, Bud Harrelson, Jerry Grote, Ed Charles, Ken Boswell, Al Weis, Art Shamsky, Ron Swoboda, Wayne Garrett, Gary Gentry, and J.C. Martin. And, of course, Agee, the popular center fielder and leadoff batter whom Gil Hodges pushed management to acquire.

"That was a very special team," Agee said. "We still enjoy getting together, playing the game."

And they're more than happy to talk about that wondrous summer in which they shocked the sports world and became the "Miracle Mets."

"People talk about a miracle," Agee said. "I don't know if it was a miracle, but no one could ever duplicate what we did in '69. I still get letters from all over the country from people asking about the '69 Mets."

Agee was a vital cog in the Mets' success in '69. Playing 149 games, he hit .271 with 26 home runs and 76 RBIs. But what most fans ask about are his two diving catches, robbing Paul Blair and Elrod Hendricks, in Game 3 of the World Series against the Orioles.

"When I made those catches," he said, "I never thought people would still be talking about it 25 years later."

Tonight, however, the topic of conversation will be Agee's bat, not his glove. The upper-deck shot was, he said, the longest home run of his career.

"I remember it was a fastball, low and in, and I just kind of golfed it up there," Agee said. "I don't know if the wind got hold of it or what, but it just kept going and going. I never saw one hit that far."

Met announcer Bob Murphy, who will be inducted into the Baseball Hall Fame in Cooperstown this summer, said the memory of Agee's homer has faded with time. But he does remember wondering if the ball would actually reach the upper deck.

"It was the first one hit up there, but there's no way I can remember the seat where it landed," Murphy said. "That was too many years ago … and I can't see that far.

Tommie Agee bats against the Pittsburgh Pirates in September 1969. The starting center fielder for the "Miracle Mets" led the team with 26 home runs and 76 RBIs. (Getty Images)

"Like so many things back then, we didn't make a big deal of it. There was no tale of the tape, so no one knew how far it went. What made it so surprising was that he was able to drop it in up there. There really isn't much room up there in fair territory."

Murphy said Agee proved he could hit with power, which is why Hodges made him a leadoff man. "Gil liked Tommie's combination of speed and power because with his pitching staff, an early one-run lead might stand up," Murphy said.

Agee, though, said he wasn't really a power hitter. "I'd hit one now and then," he said.

So how does he explain his rocket into the upper deck?

"After what I went through in '68," he said, "it was like all that anxiety from '68 came out in one swing."

Cleon Jones

Born: August 4, 1942
Height: 6'0" **Weight:** 185 lbs
Bats: Right **Throws:** Left

	Games	Ave	Hits	HR	RBI	SB
Mets (1963-75)	1,201	.281	1,188	93	521	91
Career (1963-76)	1,213	.281	1,196	93	524	91

'69 Was Divine Outfielder Recalls Never-Dull Career

August 4, 1986
By Pete Coutros

Before they took out the grass and put in the squeeze-dry carpet, rain-outs were the bane of baseball writers. All that space to fill and no hits, runs, or errors with which to fill it. On days like these, guys like Cleon Jones came in handy.

Cleon was the scribes' rainy-day friend, and they knew where he could be found. In the eye of the storm, of course. The things he did, or was alleged to have done, was grist for a lot of mills.

"I had problems with everyone," says Cleon, looking back on a troubled time. "If I were in the game today, I'd be accepted more readily. They make allowances now. You can be different and not get hung for it."

One attitude that made Cleon something other than one of the Jones boys was his intense dislike of batting practice. Where most batters, especially the .220 hitters, can't wait to get in the cage and rip at serves begging to be ripped, Cleon regarded BP as nuisance.

"When I needed batting practice, I took it. But when I was going good, I couldn't see myself hitting a lot of balls that were laid in there straight as an arrow," says Jones, whose bad underpinnings made him yearn for the comfort of the dugout pine while others were hauling ash to the batting cage.

One of Jones' more memorable confrontations was with his boss. That was the day Gil Hodges strode out to left field personally to haul Cleon back to the dugout.

"We were playing Houston and one of their players slapped one down into the corner in left field, and I knew there was no way I could keep the guy from getting a double, so I didn't go tearing after the ball," says Cleon. "Besides, I had a bum ankle, and I didn't want to make it worse on that field, which was full of puddles. When I explained this to Gil, he thought I should come out of the game. It looked like he was trying to embarrass me, but that's not how it really was."

In May 1975, Jones *was* embarrassed by Met management. This time even Cleon thought it was blatant.

After being discovered in a severe state of undress with a similarly unfettered woman in a van on a street in St. Petersburg, Jones was made to apologize to Met fans by M. Donald Grant, the club's chairman of the board. M. Donald was a stodgy sort who probably had reservations about stripping before stepping into the shower.

Hundreds of players and thousands of fans, and maybe even a board chairman, had comported themselves in some indelicate fashion without having to stand before a slew of cameras, their spouse at their side, to declare their mea culpas.

Time being the great healer, Cleon bears no animosity toward his former employers, choosing instead to remember how wonderful it was to be a Met when they amazed everyone, themselves included, in the Miracle Year of 1969.

"I suppose I had a lot better days than the last day of the '69 Series, but I can't remember anything that gave me a bigger thrill than that game, especially the way it ended."

The way it ended was that Davey Johnson, who was playing second base for the Orioles, got under a Jerry Koosman serve and lofted it into left field. Jones drifted back close to the warning track, pounded his glove twice, and then pocketed the ball to make the "miracle" official.

"Davey said he thought he'd hit a long, towering drive which was gone for sure, but I remember it as a lazy fly ball drifting into left field," says Jones.

Jones also had provided the Mets with their first run of the game, riding in on Donn Clendenon's homer after reaching base by being hit on the shoe. It took Hodges displaying a ball with shoe polish on it to convince the home plate ump that Cleon should be awarded first base.

It wasn't the first time Cleon Jones put his foot in it, or the last time. Just the best time.

Now, Jones lives in Mobile, Ala., with his wife, Angela, daughter, Anjie, and son, Cleon Jr., and lets the good times roll in the replays of his mind.

Cleon Jones was a starting outfielder for the Mets from 1966 to 1974. He led the 1969 World Series champions with a .340 batting average. (Getty Images)

Keith Hernandez

Born: October 20, 1953
Height: 6'0" **Weight:** 180 lbs
Bats: Left **Throws:** Left

	Games	Ave	Hits	HR	RBI	SB
Mets (1983–89)	880	.297	939	80	468	17
Career (1974–90)	2,088	.296	2,182	162	1,071	98

Killer Keith Has Eye of the Tiger

Hernandez Approaches Hitting Like a Chess Game

September 19, 1986
By Bob Klapisch

It starts with his eyes. The moment the ball leaves the pitcher's hand, Keith Hernandez is looking for seams. In what direction are they spinning? How fast? To a career .300 hitter, the answers mean everything.

"The slider has a tight, circular spin. The better the slider, the smaller the spin," Hernandez said. "John Montefusco had the tightest spin I ever saw. His slider was unbelievable. Joe Niekro, on the other hand, had a real wide spin.

"The curveball's spin rotates head over the top, like the earth on its axis. The better the curveball, the faster the spin. Mike Krukow, Bert Blyleven, Don Sutton…they make the ball spin like a top. Obviously the worse the curveball, the slower the spin."

A fastball? "Nothing special. It's a straight spin, the easiest to pick up."

A split-finger fastball? "Tough pitch, because it looks like a fastball, then drops in a hurry. The key," Hernandez said, "is to wait until the last moment and be quick."

Be quick. That's been Hernandez's calling card for 12 seasons. At 32, he shows no sign of an aging bat. He even talks about playing until he's 40.

Despite his well-publicized, off-season problems—a $135,000 fine and mandatory, random drug-testing imposed by Peter Ueberroth last March—Hernandez is having his best year since 1979.

He's hitting .312 with 76 RBIs and leads the NL in on-base percentage (.414) and walks (88). After a June-July slump that saw his average dip into the .280s, Hernandez is currently on a 57-for-146 (.390) tear over his last 39 games. Some are even saying that he—and not Gary Carter—is the National League's MVP.

Hernandez never mentions the Pittsburgh drug trial—not ever. But he does admit, "This spring was the most intense, most stressful time in my life. But I knew I'd come through it. I'm a .300 hitter."

How? Why? Don Mattingly, who admits to a keen interest in Hernandez, once said, "I watch Keith at the plate and wonder, 'How does he ever hit the inside pitch? That stance… I've never seen anything like it."

Hernandez used to have a Mickey Mantle poster on his wall during his high school days. For years he copied the Mick's stance. Now, Hernandez's hands are too high, his butt too far out. How does he hit .300? Simple. With keen eyes, a calculating mind, and the first law of hitting: Be quick.

"I've made a career keeping my bat level on the inside fastball," Hernandez said. "I have an inside-out swing, which gives me the ability to hit the ball hard to left field. My dad taught me that. He made me swing level on high, inside pitches.

"I watch Mattingly on TV once in a while. I wonder, 'With that crouch, how can he hit the high pitch?' But he does. He keeps his bat level, which is the sign of a great hitter."

Good hitters not only react, they think. "The key to Hernandez's success is that he thinks along with the pitcher," Tom Seaver said. "I play more mind games with him than almost any hitter I've ever faced."

It's more than guessing, Hernandez said. He plays chess. Can a hitter set up a pitcher? Absolutely. "Pitchers have patterns. They all do," Hernandez said. "You know why? Because pitchers cannot relate to hitting. They have no idea what goes through a hitter's mind.

"The best pitchers are the ones who are good hitters themselves. Knowing the catcher helps, too, because catchers usually call what they can't hit."

Hernandez learned about fooling pitchers from the reclusive George Hendrick, now a California Angel and a teammate of Keith's in St. Louis. Hendrick—a gifted curveball hitter—would deliberately look bad on an early-inning breaking ball…so he would see it later in a tight situation.

Pitchers are egomaniacs that way. Once they succeed, they rarely change. "That's why George would fall to his knees, swinging so hard through a pitch," Hernandez said. "Because he knew he'd see the same pitch later.

"I use the same idea: One example was against [the Cubs'] Dick Ruthven one day in

Keith Hernandez grabs a pickoff attempt as San Diego's Marvell Wynne slides back into first base safely during a 1986 game at Shea Stadium. Hernandez won 11 Gold Gloves in his career. (Getty Images)

1984. First three times up, he was painting the outside corner on me. Fourth time up, I got in the box, made sure Jody [catcher Davis] saw me get an inch from the plate.

Obviously, I was looking inside fastball…which I got and hit over the wall. That's how I set him up."

Hernandez's dossier says he uses a 34½-inch, 32-ounce C-721 Louisville Slugger. His strike-zone sweet-spot is down the middle, or three inches inside either corner. He feels comfortable with John Denny, and can't be jammed by Floyd Youmans' heat.

His five toughest pitchers? John Candelaria, Kevin Gross, Don Sutton, Larry McWilliams, and Steve Rogers.

"I love to hit. I've never lost that love," Hernandez said. "I don't even think I've lost anything from '79 [when he won the NL's batting crown with a .344 average]. My goal is going to be 3,000 hits. I've got a shot."

All he needs is sharp eyes.

Above: Keith Hernandez hits a three-run home run against the St. Louis Cardinals in 1987. He hit a career-high 18 home runs that season. (AP Images)

Right: Keith Hernandez fields the ball at Wrigley Field. Hernandez is referred to by some as the greatest defensive first baseman of all time. (Getty Images)

Darryl Strawberry

Born: March 12, 1962
Height: 6'6" **Weight:** 190 lbs
Bats: Left **Throws:** Left

	Games	Ave	Hits	HR	RBI	SB
Mets (1983–90)	1,109	.263	1,025	252	733	191
Career (1983–99)	1,583	.259	1,401	335	1,000	221

Straw Stirs Again
Franchise's Biggest Star Returns to Organization

March 8, 2005
By Mark Hale

It all looked so natural. Blue cap, blue No. 18 jersey, gray pants, big smile.

Maybe it's because after 15 years, Darryl Strawberry was finally back home.

Strawberry, the greatest position player in Mets history, officially returned to the team yesterday to work as a special instructor. As he strolled around Tradition Field—which opened in 1988, right in the man's prime, making it practically The House That Straw Built—it felt like the triumphant return of a baseball son who had gone adrift.

"This is where really everything happened for me," Strawberry said. "My best days of playing were here."

It was the first time Strawberry joined the Mets in any capacity since he left the team after the 1990 season to sign with the Dodgers. From there, he spent time with L.A., the Giants, and the Yankees, winning three World Series with the Bombers.

Through it all, though, Strawberry remained forever associated with the Mets, who drafted him first overall in 1980 and watched him thrill Shea fans for eight seasons. He remains the franchise's all-time leader in homers, RBIs, extra-base hits, and runs, but even those gaudy rankings fail to provide evidence of his flair for the spectacular. As GM Omar Minaya said in recalling the '86 champion Mets, "He was the star-appeal guy."

"The best," Doug Mientkiewicz, a fan of that '86 team, said of Straw. "The best of his time."

Fifteen years later, the best is back here to help. Strawberry will be in camp for about a week, working with the organization's outfielders.

But Strawberry also has a bigger message than how to track fly balls and play the corners. His checkered history of drug and financial problems caused him to waste part of his dazzling talent, and he's determined not to let that happen to anybody else.

"I think young players today need to make the right decisions," Strawberry said. "I had to learn the hard way. My thing is about young people making the right decisions and choices. Don't make some of the mistakes I made in life."

Added Strawberry, "It's not about swinging a bat for me anymore. It's about who I can help."

There's no question Strawberry can help out with younger players. Just ask Derek Jeter, who like Straw, was once a young star emerging in New York.

"Straw's one of the best teammates you'll ever have," Jeter said yesterday. "The thing I remember about Straw is my second year at the beginning of spring training. There's nobody in here. Straw called me over, sat me down, talked to me for 15–20 minutes. Basically talking about New York, someone in a similar situation. He could relate to what I was going through."

Asked whether things might have been different for him if he hadn't left the Mets, Strawberry admitted it likely would have. "But no regrets," he said. "Life is life."

Strawberry, who has also overcome colon cancer, said his health is good now. And these days, he spends most of his time with his kids—19-year-old D.J., who plays hoops for Maryland, and 10-year-old Jordan. Said Straw, "It feels good to be a dad."

As for whether this week-long experience will leave him hungry for a bigger role in the organization, Strawberry isn't sure yet. For now, it was enough for him to simply introduce himself to players who now occupy his former locker room.

"It's these guys' time. It's not my time," he said. "My time is over. I've done what I had to do as far as my performance playing baseball. It's these guys' time and I just hope I can inspire these guys about winning."

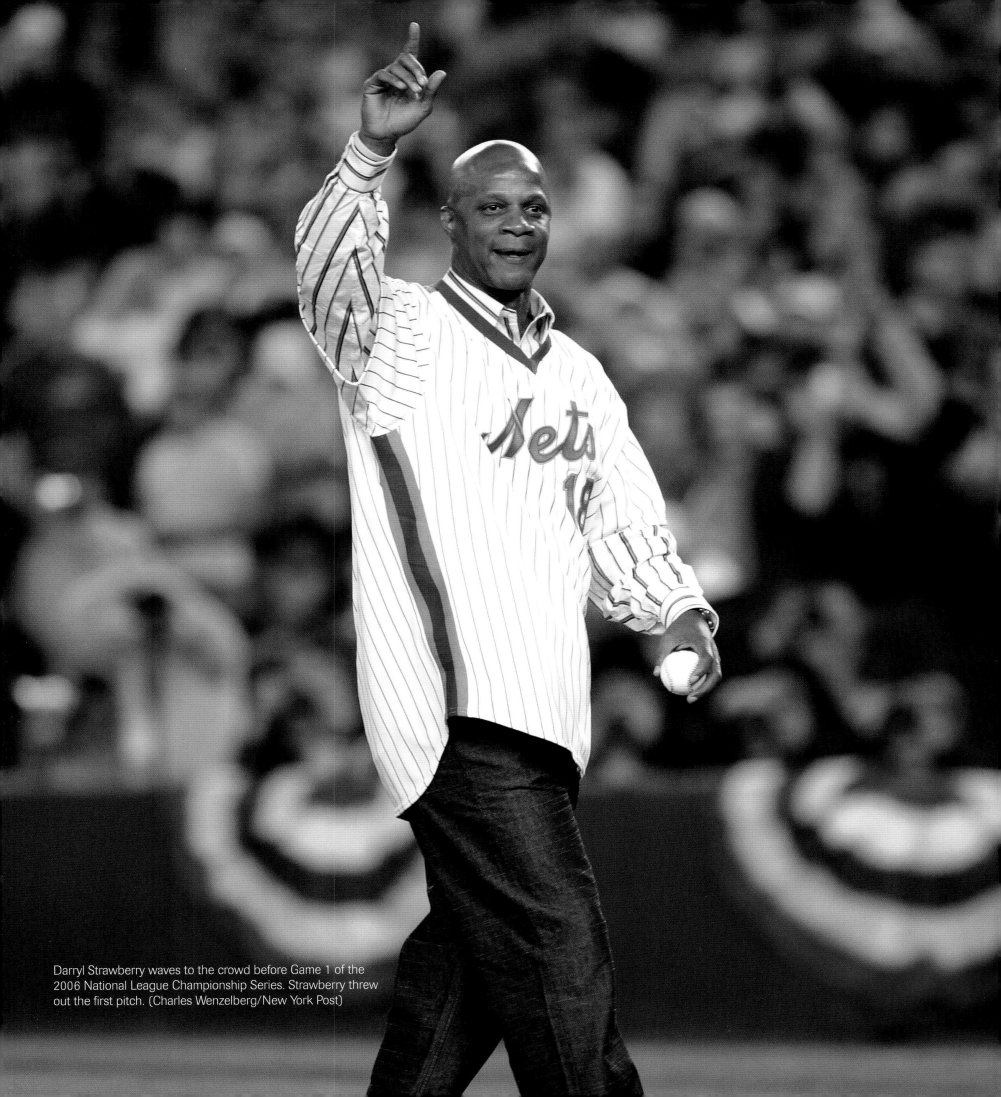

Darryl Strawberry waves to the crowd before Game 1 of the 2006 National League Championship Series. Strawberry threw out the first pitch. (Charles Wenzelberg/New York Post)

Darryl Strawberry watches the flight of a ball he hit against the Cubs at Chicago's Wrigley Field in 1988. Strawberry tied his career high with 39 home runs in 1988, leading the National League. (Getty Images)

Batting against the San Francisco Giants at Candlestick Park during his final season as a Met in 1990, Darryl Strawberry awaits the pitch. Strawberry hit 252 of his 335 career home runs in a Mets uniform. (Getty Images)

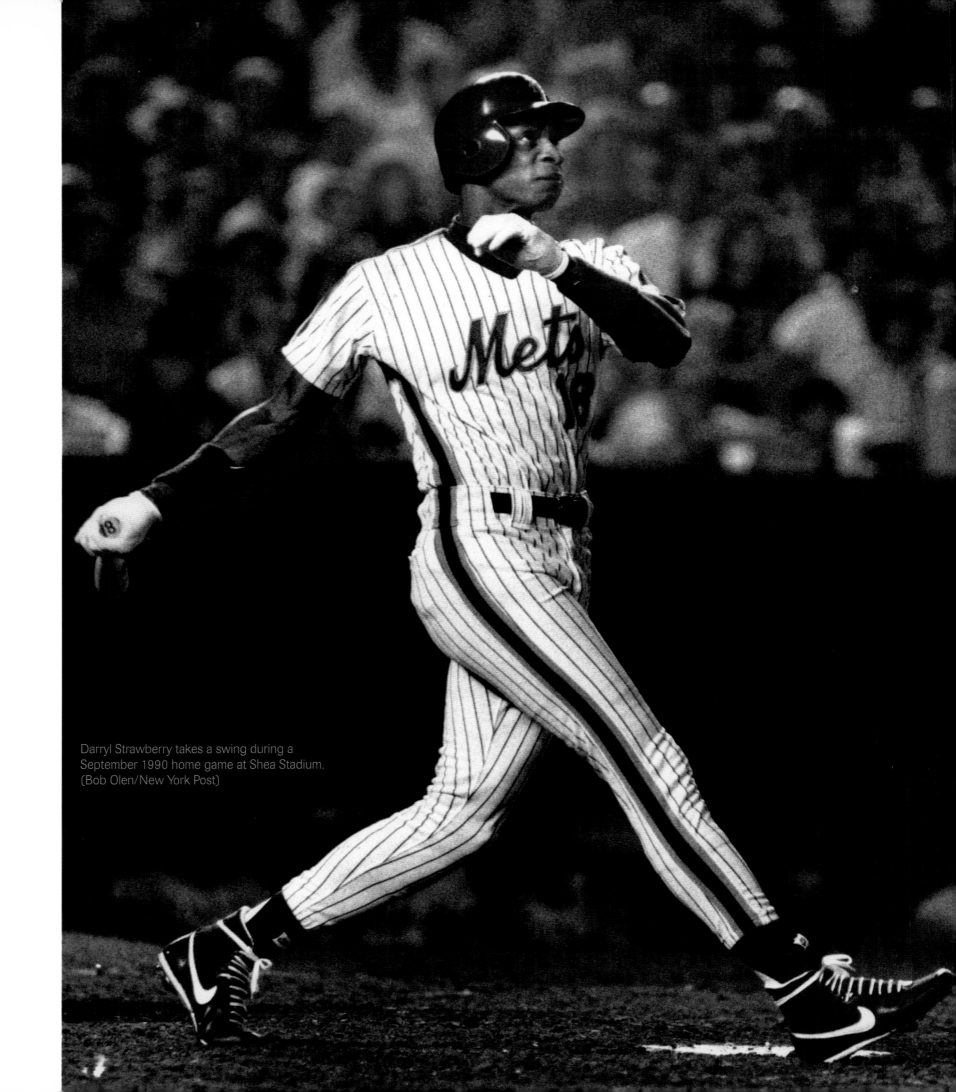

Darryl Strawberry takes a swing during a
September 1990 home game at Shea Stadium.
(Bob Olen/New York Post)

Darryl Strawberry

Darryl Strawberry reacts after throwing out the first pitch on Opening Day at Citi Field in 2010. Since the mid-2000s, Strawberry has been involved with the Mets organization. (AP Images)

Dwight Gooden

Born: November 16, 1964
Height: 6'2" Weight: 190 lbs
Bats: Right Throws: Right

	W-L	ERA	IP	Hits	BB	K	CG
Mets (1984-94)	157-85	3.10	2,169.2	1,898	651	1,875	67
Career (1984-2000)	194-112	3.51	2,800.2	2,564	954	2,293	68

Doc of the Town Pitcher Captured City's Heart in 1984

March 28, 2007
By Mike Vaccaro

The greatest phenom in the history of New York baseball was able to ease his way into the spotlight 23 years ago, to enter the city's baseball cauldron via the back door, a path that's not only no longer passable, it's no longer possible. The world of 2007 simply would never permit Dwight Gooden to sneak up on us. Or on anyone else, for that matter.

"We'd heard about this kid with a live arm, and of course we'd seen him here and there, but we didn't know just what we were in for," is the way Keith Hernandez described the Great Gooden Arrival of 1984. "If there was a lot of hype, I don't remember it."

You can't remember it because it wasn't there. The first time Dwight Gooden took the mound at Shea Stadium, on April 19, 1984, there were exactly 10,705 people in the stands. Gooden pitched five innings against the Montreal Expos. He threw 118 pitches. He struck out seven, got a no-decision, the Mets won the game later on, and he would sheepishly admit, "I couldn't find my fastball until I got loose and broke a sweat."

There were a lot of reasons for the great yawn that greeted Gooden's home unveiling. The Mets were just emerging from a seven-year stretch of woeful baseball in which they'd surrendered the town back to the Yankees without a fight. It was cold that night, which explains why Gooden, a perspirer of epic proportions, couldn't break a sweat. Mostly, though, we still existed in a word-of-mouth world.

But once the word got around, once it spread, once it infected the baseball sensibilities of baseball's most sensible city?

Well, we won't see anything like that anymore, either. Whenever Philip Hughes makes his first start at Yankee Stadium, nothing he does will be a surprise. We already know too much about him. Same with Mike Pelfrey, who made his debut last summer in the second game of a doubleheader with the Marlins, two days before the All-Star break, and he was already a familiar name to all but the most peripheral Mets fan.

That is why the Gooden of 1984 stands alone as the singular baseball phenomenon in the history of New York City. Lou Gehrig was overshadowed by Babe Ruth as a rookie, and Joe DiMaggio was overshadowed by Gehrig. Mickey Mantle got himself farmed out to Kansas City as a rookie. Tom Seaver joined a baseball sitcom (and only 5,005 people bothered to come to Shea for his debut on April 13, 1967). Even Derek Jeter, as splendid as he was as a rook, never captured the city's attention, or its imagination, the way Gooden did in '84.

History tells us that 1984 wasn't Gooden's pinnacle; that would come a year later, when his numbers (24–4, 1.53 ERA, 268 strikeouts) became a part of every Mets fan's permanent mental database. But Gooden the rookie actually struck out eight more batters in almost 60 fewer innings. He not only became an instant attraction at Shea, he invented must-see TV when Jerry Seinfeld was still playing Dangerfield's.

Upstairs at Shea, in Section 44, a couple of young fans from North Haledon, N.J., named Dennis Scalzitti and Leo Avolio started bringing 27 placards with the letter "K" stenciled on them. They were two of the 10,705 there the very first night. The "K Korner" was born then and there.

"I missed one game in three years," Scalzitti told me a few years ago. "Hey, I would have gone anyway, made the trip over from Jersey as much as I could, just because when he pitched you never knew when he was going to do something you'd never seen before."

What came later on, the sad decline, that's always going to be a part of the Dwight Gooden story. It's telling that his final career numbers, 194–112, 3.51 ERA, 2,293 strikeouts, by any measure an above-average career inspire sadness, because those who favor "at this pace" conversations can still remember that, after his first five years, Gooden was "on pace" to win 364 games and strike out 4,268 over what was sure to be a 20-year career for the ages. It never worked out quite that way. Part of the story.

But 1984 will always be a part of the story, too, the best part, the part we're always looking to replicate every time the next live young arm shows up in the big city, the one we'll never be able to copy ever again. For so many reasons, the most compelling of which is this: when they called Dwight Gooden a once-in-a-lifetime pitcher all those years ago? They were right.

Dwight Gooden winds up to throw a pitch during a 1988 game at Shea Stadium. (Getty Images)

Dwight Gooden enjoys himself on the Wrigley Field mound early in his career. (Getty Images)

Mets fans Dennis Scalzitti and Leo Avolio regularly posted "K" cards along the Shea Stadium upper deck when Dwight Gooden pitched for the Mets. The duo even traveled to away games on occasion. Above, they put up the 14th "K" after Gooden struck out 14 San Francisco Giants at Candlestick Park on May 30, 1985. At left, Scalzitti and Avolio (right) meet with Gooden in August 1984. (AP Images)

Opposite page: Dwight Gooden looks on from the dugout as the Mets blow a three-run eighth-inning lead to the St. Louis Cardinals on September 16, 1992, effectively eliminating the Mets from the National League East playoff picture. The 1992 season marked the first time in Gooden's career that he posted a losing record. (Bob Olen/New York Post)

Left: Dwight Gooden (top) and Darryl Strawberry pose together at Citi Field in January 2010 after it was announced that the two 1980s stars would be inducted into the Mets Hall of Fame. (AP Images)

Gary Carter

Born: April 8, 1954
Height: 6'2" **Weight:** 205 lbs
Bats: Right **Throws:** Right

	Games	Ave	Hits	HR	RBI	SB
Mets (1985-89)	600	.249	542	89	349	2
Career (1974-92)	2,296	.262	2,092	324	1,225	39

The Kid Catcher's Not Easy to Keep Off the Field

October 6, 1986
By Bob Klapisch

Looking at his knee assaults the eyes. Scars, nasty cuts, swollen bruises. You're almost thankful Gary Carter covers it with protective tape. Snip, cut, wrap—every day. Such is life without knee cartilage.

Hours before his first batting-practice swing, Carter is standing on the trainer's table. Standing? He's there getting his right knee bandaged by trainer Steve Garland.

Garland has removed one of the overhead tiles so Carter's head will fit through the low ceiling. Fifteen minutes, sometimes 20, Carter stares into darkness. These are slices of a handicap no one sees.

Look at Carter's knee and you wonder: how did he avoid The Final Collision? Carter knows that another serious injury would be disastrous. One wrong slide and…Davey Johnson shudders. But incredibly, Gary Carter survived 1986 without a scratch on the knee. Amazing.

"I was always aware what kind of damage could've been done. I never forget that," he said. "But I never woke up thinking, 'Today's the day. I'm through.' I played hard and took my chances. That's really the only way I can play."

Critics tell us Carter, 32, is a TV player: false hustle, manufactured enthusiasm. But Carter does play hard and, regardless of his sub-.250 batting average, led the Mets in RBIs all summer. In fact, his RBI-to-at-bat ratio was among the NL's best.

Do his numbers merit an MVP award? Probably not, since Mike Schmidt made a late-season surge. But Carter has made invaluable contributions to the Mets. He handled the pitching staff. He threw out runners. He acted as Sid Fernandez's caretaker.

Actually, Carter's batting average was his only obstacle to the MVP. He admits, "My average was somewhat lower than I would've liked. But I think I was productive on the whole. I'm happy with the season I've had."

Ironically, the only serious injury he suffered this year was at first base. Carter remembers diving for an Aug. 16 ground ball against the Cardinals. Snap. This time it happened—a partially torn ligament in his left thumb.

The Mets were 16½ games in front, so Carter's two-week absence could be absorbed. But this was the injury the Mets had always feared. It wasn't the knee, but the point was the same. Who was his caddy?

His name was Ed Hearn, a quiet, almost shy 25-year-old rookie. Hearn openly admitted: "No one replaces Gary Carter. I don't care if you're Tony Pena." The collapse never came, however. The Mets were 11–3 in Carter's absence and had increased their lead to 19 games by the time he returned.

Carter could've taken a two-week sabbatical—show up at the park, dabble with the whirlpool, become invisible. No one would have said a word. In fact, Hearn said: "Maybe this is what Gary needed. I'm afraid he was burning himself out."

But Carter behaved like a caged animal. Two days after his hand was placed in a cast, he said: "I think I probably could play if I had to." Within four days, he was hovering near the batting cage, bat in hand. Johnson said, "I tried to get him to take a few days off, but Gary wouldn't listen. He was driving me nuts."

By the seventh day, Carter was taking batting practice again. He was out of prison. "Another couple days of that," he said, "and I would've gone out of my mind. I mean that. If I ever have to spend a lot of time on the disabled list…well, someone will have to shoot me, like they destroy horses that are suffering."

Carter was smiling, but he wasn't kidding. He is hopelessly addicted to being a Met. Is his enthusiasm genuine? Say this much for Carter: not even an out-of-service knee diminishes his love for baseball. Only one ingredient is missing.

"This has been such an unbelievable year," Carter said, "that winning a World Series seems like the most fitting way to end it."

Gary Carter is all smiles during a Mets game against the Chicago Cubs at Wrigley Field. One of baseball's great catchers, Carter starred for the Mets from 1985 to 1989. (Getty Images)

Howard Johnson

Born: November 29, 1960
Height: 5'11" **Weight:** 178 lbs
Bats: Both **Throws:** Right

	Games	Ave	Hits	HR	RBI	SB
Mets (1985–93)	1,154	.251	997	192	629	202
Career (1982–95)	1,531	.249	1,229	228	760	231

Power From Both Sides

HoJo Reaches RBI Goal to Cap Stellar Season

October 1, 1989
By John Harper

It was the last hurdle, and Howard Johnson wanted desperately to clear it. He's done it all this season, earning the respect throughout baseball that he always thought he deserved.

But it wasn't until he hit a three-run home run Friday night and went over the 100-RBI mark for the first time in his career that HoJo could sit back and smile.

"It's definitely a relief," HoJo was saying before last night's game with the Pirates. "At least I can say I did it one time. I didn't want to get stuck on 99 again."

He'd done that in '87, and when the RBI faucet slowed to a drip in the last couple of weeks, HoJo admitted he began to worry about it—especially after the Mets were eliminated Monday night.

"I didn't like playing just for personal reasons," said HoJo. "When we got eliminated, I lost some of my intensity, and it's tough to play like that. I had been overswinging for a couple of weeks."

Fittingly, he reached his milestone against a pitcher, Jeff Robinson, who had given him a lot of trouble over the years, getting him to chase forkballs in the dirt. Friday night he told himself to relax, just make contact, the way he has all season, and he wound up taking a knee-high pitch over the wall for his 36th home run.

It was fitting because this is the season when HoJo came of age as a hitter, learned to be patient, learned to sit back on the breaking balls and trust his lightning-quick hands to handle the hard stuff.

And so it was the season he got even with his tormentors, pitchers like Orel Hershiser, Bryn Smith, and Robinson, who had always gotten him to chase the curve balls in the past.

He took each of them deep, Smith twice in 1988. But the beauty of his season is not so much in his home runs, but in his all-around numbers. He went into last night's game with a .285 average, 101 RBIs, 101 runs scored, a club-record 42 doubles, and 40 stolen bases.

He'd pretty much given up on the idea of becoming the NL's first 40-40 man, he said, when he didn't hit any home runs on the 10-game road trip that ended last week. But that was never so much his goal as the idea of becoming a complete hitter.

"Personally, I've achieved everything I wanted to achieve," he said after getting the RBIs. "I'm probably proudest of the 40 doubles, because to do that means you're making consistent contact, you're hitting with some power, and you're stretching a lot of singles into doubles."

His only regret, of course, is that none of it was enough to put the Mets over the top this season. He has always been a tireless worker, and with his success this year, overcoming his disastrous '88 playoff showing, the trade rumors, and his throwing problems, HoJo has emerged as a quiet leader among the Mets and perhaps the No. 3 hitter for the '90s.

There are plenty of questions to be answered over the winter, of course, and one key decision may well involve HoJo. If the Mets decide to move Gregg Jefferies away from second base, and management seems to be leaning that way, HoJo probably would be moved to make room at third base.

First base is a possibility, maybe even the outfield. HoJo is aware of the possibilities, and though he makes it clear he'd like to stay at third, he says he'll move if it's best for the Mets.

"I'll do whatever it takes for us to win," said HoJo. "I'm not going to rock the boat. I understand that some people aren't happy with Jefferies at second base, that his progress there has been slow. But he's improved a lot lately.

"I think the club will do a lot of evaluating this winter, and once they decide what they want to do, they'll probably talk to me about it. I played a little first base one year in the Instructional League. I could play it, but I wouldn't be great. I played a little outfield years ago, but I'd prefer to stay in the infield."

One thing is for sure. HoJo doesn't have to worry about staying in New York anymore. The Mets will be rebuilding around him.

David Cone

Born: January 2, 1963
Height: 6'1" Weight: 180 lbs
Bats: Left Throws: Right

	W–L	ERA	IP	Hits	BB	K	CG
Mets (1987–91, 2003)	81–51	3.13	1,209.1	1,011	431	1,172	34
Career (1986–2003)	194–126	3.46	2,898.2	2,504	1,137	2,668	56

Steal of the Century
How the Mets Corralled Cone in Royal Heist

May 27, 1988
By John Harper

In a New York baseball sky already cluttered with stars, David Cone has made an impression as unmistakable as a streaking comet.

Besides blinding the National League with a 6–0 record and a 1.75 ERA, he is pitching with a boldness that already has set off sparks. Just ask Pedro Guerrero.

Cone is the definition of a phenom in 1988. Except phenoms are born, not traded.

Cone, 25, has the face of an altar boy but the instincts of a pit bull. He was a gift to the Mets from the Royals.

The price paid, as you surely know, was catcher Ed Hearn, then 26, and right-hander Rick Anderson, then 30. Hearn has been sidelined by a rotator-cuff injury, while Anderson, a junkballer, has been unable to escape Triple-A.

In Kansas City, the media is calling the trade the worst in Royal history. Keith Hernandez, rarely guilty of overstatement, recently called it the steal of the century.

But how? Why? Joe McIlvaine allows himself a small smile as he recalls details of the March 1987 trade. Even now, McIlvaine wonders how the Mets pried loose a prospect like Cone.

"It's very unusual to get the top pitching prospect in an organization," McIlvaine said this week. "Frankly, I was surprised, because our reports on him were so strong. It's rare when you get universal agreement on a player, but we had it."

It was the Royals, in search of a starting catcher, who opened the door to the trade. McIlvaine recalls a KC scout asking during the '86 winter whom the Mets might want in return for Hearn, Gary Carter's backup.

McIlvaine, figuring there was no harm in asking, mentioned Cone. When the scout, whom McIlvaine would not identify, didn't firmly and immediately rule it out, McIlvaine felt as if he'd been dealt a full house in a high-stakes poker game. Now it was up to him to play the hand and play it hard.

He puts it this way: "I had a smell that I could get this guy, and I really went after him."

McIlvaine spent hours on the phone that winter with John Schuerholz, the Royals' trigger man, whose style, says McIlvaine, "is brutally direct. You can be forthright with him." Schuerholz knew that Cone, a third-round draft choice in 1981 and a local boy from KC, had potential. He went 16–3 in A ball in '82, and although he tore up a knee the following season, Cone had recovered and was moving up the organizational ladder.

McIlvaine, however, held the upper hand. For one thing, the Mets were well-stocked world champs. For another, neither Hearn nor Anderson, the players Schuerholz had pegged, figured in the Mets' plans, while the Royals clearly needed a catcher.

So McIlvaine held firm through the winter and most of spring training. The Royals offered almost every other young pitcher in their organization, but McIlvaine wouldn't budge.

Cone or no deal.

The Mets had become sold on Cone the previous winter. He had already shown potential as a starter in the minors, demonstrating a live arm and good breaking ball. And then he had excelled as a short reliever in Puerto Rico, offering a glimpse of his toughness.

"Really good guts," McIlvaine remembers thinking.

The Royals, meanwhile, were high on Cone but not convinced he was a can't-miss blue-chipper. After missing an entire season in '83 with a Bernard King–like knee injury—suffered when he made a tag at the plate following a wild pitch—he struggled with control in Double-A (8–12, 4.27 ERA) and again in Triple-A (9–14, 4.67).

Cone was 23 years old and just beginning to put his game back together. Then in '86 he was up and down between Kansas City and Triple-A Omaha, spotty as a major league reliever. He appeared in only 11 games, pitching 22⅓ innings, striking out 21 while walking 13 and allowing 14 earned runs.

"I was never really given a chance," says Cone.

As spring training approached, Cone was aware of trade rumors. But he didn't believe them. As the season neared, however, Schuerholz was more and more certain he had to get a young catcher. Hearn had shown potential, filling in nicely for an injured Carter in August of '86.

David Cone throws a pitch during an August 1987 home game at Shea Stadium. Acquired from Kansas City for catcher Ed Hearn at the end of spring training in 1987, Cone went 20-3 with a 2.22 earned run average in 1988. (Getty Images)

Finally, Schuerholz, already armed with a solid pitching staff (Bret Saberhagen, Charlie Leibrandt, Mark Gubicza, Danny Jackson, Bud Black), felt he had to gamble. He called McIlvaine and said he'd surrender Cone.

McIlvaine had won the battle of nerves.

"Their need was greater than ours," he says.

Officially, the Mets also got minor league catcher Chris Jelic and gave up Hearn, Anderson, and minor league pitcher Mauro Gozzo.

It was March 27. Only a day earlier, Royal manager Billy Gardner, not privy to Schuerholz's intentions, had named Cone as KC's fifth starter.

"Never in my wildest dreams did I expect to be traded," says Cone. "They called me in that morning and told me they were announcing the trade in five minutes. I didn't believe it.

"I had five minutes to get ready for a press conference. It was the toughest time I ever had controlling my emotions. I'd gotten my first hit the day before against John Tudor, so I told the writers the Mets obviously wanted me for my bat, and that kind of broke the tension. But it was tough."

A boyhood dream was shattered. Cone, who grew up in Kansas City, started attending Royal games when he was six years old. A championship quarterback for powerful Rockhurst High, he'd given up a football-baseball scholarship to Missouri when the Royals offered him $15,000 to sign and a guarantee to pay his college education if he didn't make it in baseball.

Now, suddenly, Cone was a Met and had less than a week to impress them or go back to Triple-A. It didn't take long. The first batter he faced was Jack Clark. Cone struck him out on three pitches.

"Two fastballs and a Laredo slider," says Cone.

Immediately, the Mets sensed they had something special. Cone's 1987 season was interrupted for 2½ months when he broke his right index finger attempting to bunt against the Giants' Atlee Hammaker. But now, after a whirlwind month that has seen Cone step into the rotation for injured Rick Aguilera, the way Lou Gehrig once filled in for Wally Pipp, there is little doubt.

If the Royals underestimated anything about Cone, it was the grit that enabled him to come back from major reconstructive knee surgery and the poise and competitiveness that go back to being a high school quarterback. Back then, he was a 6-foot, 170-pound kid who didn't think he was good enough to be a pro athlete. He was contemplating a career as a sportswriter.

Now he considers his move to the rotation, his 6-0 record, and says: "This is what I wanted. I want to squeeze everything I can out of it. The trade has been a blessing; it really has."

As Met fans might say, amen.

The Managers

Gil Hodges receives an assist from Yogi Berra as he puts on the Mets cap after being named manager for the 1968 season. Flanking the pair are Mets team president Bing Devine, left, and bullpen coach Joe Pignatano. Hodges managed the Mets to the 1969 World Series championship. After Hodges' sudden death before the 1972 season, Berra took over and led the Mets' 1973 National League Championship squad.
(AP Images)

The roll call of men in charge of the Mets' lineup cards during the franchise's first half century includes a collection of names well known to any fan of New York baseball. Whether chasing the pennant or fighting to stay out of the National League East cellar, the Mets' first 20 managers were anything but dull.

When George Weiss was tabbed as the Mets' first team president, he hired then-71-year-old Casey Stengel to manage the expansion team. In 12 seasons together as general manager and manager of the Yankees, Weiss and Stengel's teams won 10 American League pennants and seven World Series before the duo was forced to retire after the 1960 season. Stengel's 175–404 record in three-plus seasons with the expansion Mets was a far cry from the success of his Yankees teams, but the "Old Perfessor" succeeded in drawing fans and providing such unforgettable lines as, "I got one [catcher] that can throw but can't catch, one that can catch but can't throw, and one who can hit but can't do either."

Stengel retired after breaking his hip during the 1965 season and was succeeded by Wes Westrum, who posted a .375 winning percentage over parts of three seasons. For the 1968 campaign, Gil Hodges was tabbed to manage the Mets. The former Brooklyn Dodgers star first baseman and original Met—who hit the first home run in franchise history in 1962—led the Mets to a respectable 73–89 finish in his first season, the expansion team's highest win total in its first seven seasons. Hodges' true triumph, however, came in 1969 as his "Miracle Mets" won 100 games and captured the World Series title. Hodges' Mets finished in third place in both 1970 and 1971, with identical 83–79 records. Then, just before the start of the 1972 season, Hodges suffered a fatal heart attack on April 2, 1972, just two days short of his 48th birthday.

Casey Stengel bids farewell to the Polo Grounds on September 18, 1963. The Mets' first manager provided fans with colorful assessments of his teams, including, "The only thing worse than a Mets game is a Mets doubleheader." (AP Images)

Yogi Berra, who finished his Hall of Fame playing career with the Mets as a player-coach in 1965 and served on the team's coaching staff from that point forward, was tasked with the challenge of succeeding Hodges in 1972. Berra's tenure in the Mets dugout included the acquisition of Willie Mays in 1972. In 1973, the Mets stood in last place midway through their season when manager Berra uttered his famous proclamation: "It ain't over till it's over." The Mets fought back to win the National League East with an 82–79 record and upset the favored Cincinnati Reds for the pennant before falling to the Oakland Athletics in the World Series. Yogi managed the Mets through the middle of the 1975 season.

Joe Frazier, who had managed the Mets' Triple-A team, was promoted to the big league job in 1976 and led the Mets to a third-place finish. Frazier was let go during the 1977 season as the Mets entered a seven-year period of futility. The Amazins failed to reach the 70-win mark each year from 1977 through 1983, never finishing higher than fifth place in the National League East. If nothing else, this period served as a training ground for a manager who would later become one of the game's greatest. Joe Torre, wrapping up his playing career as the Mets' first baseman, was named player-manager early in the 1977 season, succeeding Frazier. Torre managed the team through the end of the strike-shortened 1981 campaign. He was replaced by longtime Baltimore Orioles pitching coach

Gil Hodges enjoys a laugh during a game against the Pittsburgh Pirates in September 1969. The former Brooklyn Dodgers first baseman and original Met managed the "Miracle Mets" to the World Series championship in 1969, the expansion team's eighth season. A heart attack claimed Hodges' life in April 1972, just before his 48th birthday. (Getty Images)

George Bamberger, who failed to reach the 70-win mark the next season with a lineup that featured Dave Kingman at first base and an aging George Foster in left field. Bamberger was fired during the 1983 season as a starting rotation led by 38-year-old Tom Seaver and 36-year-old Mike Torrez finished 68–94.

The Mets finally found success—and continuity in the dugout—in 1984 when Davey Johnson was hired. Johnson, an All-Star second baseman for the Orioles in the 1960s and 1970s, had worked up the coaching ladder in the Mets organization. His Mets won at least 90 games in each of Johnson's first five seasons, including the 108-win 1986 World Series champions and the 1988 National League East team that won 100 games before falling to the Dodgers in the playoffs. The once-dominating Mets came back to earth in 1989 and 1990 as age began to catch up with stars such as Keith Hernandez and Gary Carter, and Johnson was let go during the 1990 season. He was replaced by former Mets shortstop and longtime coach Bud Harrelson, who posted a 145–129 mark over two seasons. Jeff Torborg (1992–93) and Dallas Green (1993-96) managed the Mets through the middle of the decade, and the Mets failed to reach the .500 mark for six consecutive seasons.

Bobby Valentine, the Texas Rangers' manager from 1985 to 1992, was managing the Mets' Triple-A Norfolk team in 1996 and took over the major league club at the end of the season after Green was fired. Valentine was at the helm during the Mets' resurgence in the late 1990s and early 2000s. Consecutive 88-win seasons in 1997 and '98 were followed by National League Wild Card wins in 1999 and 2000. The Mets lost to Atlanta in the NLCS in 1999, then advanced to the World Series in 2000—losing the Subway Series to the Yankees in five games. Always a colorful character, one of Valentine's signature moments came during an interleague matchup with Toronto in 1999. After Valentine was ejected in the 12th inning for arguing a catcher's interference call against Mike Piazza, he returned to the dugout wearing a

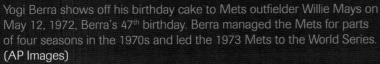

Yogi Berra shows off his birthday cake to Mets outfielder Willie Mays on May 12, 1972, Berra's 47th birthday. Berra managed the Mets for parts of four seasons in the 1970s and led the 1973 Mets to the World Series. (AP Images)

Joe Torre pitches batting practice at Shea Stadium before a 1981 game. Torre managed the Mets from 1977 through 1981. (Getty Images)

fake mustache in disguise. The incident earned Valentine a $5,000 fine and three-game suspension. Valentine was let go after a fifth-place finish in 2002. Valentine's replacement, Art Howe, fared no better as his teams finished under .500 in 2003 and 2004.

Willie Randolph was named before the 2005 season. Randolph's name was well known to New York baseball fans. He was a star second baseman for the Yankees in the 1970s and '80s and a member of the Bronx Bombers' coaching staff for 11 seasons prior to taking the Mets job. Randolph's Mets finished 83–79 in Randolph's first season. In 2006, the Mets won the National League East and tied the Yankees for the best record in the major leagues with a 97–65 record. They swept the Dodgers in the NLDS before falling to the Cardinals in seven games in the NLCS. Randolph's 2007 Mets led the National League East by seven games with 17 games to play, but finished 5–12 and lost the division to the late-surging Philadelphia Phillies. After an inconsistent start, Randolph was let go in June 2008 and replaced by Jerry Manuel. Manuel remained at the helm through the end of the 2010 season, but was let go after consecutive fourth-place finishes.

Terry Collins took over in 2011. Behind strong starts by All-Stars Jose Reyes and Carlos Beltran, the Mets were in third place with a .500 record on July 4. Only time will tell whether Collins joins Hodges, Berra, Johnson, and Valentine in the pantheon of great Mets skippers.

Bobby Valentine relays signals during a May 1999 home game against the Cincinnati Reds. Valentine managed the Mets from 1996 to 2002 and led the Amazins to the National League Championship Series in 1999 and the World Series in 2000. (Nury Hernandez/New York Post)

Willie Randolph looks on from the dugout during an August 2007 game against Florida. Randolph managed the Mets to three consecutive winning seasons. The Mets were within one game of the World Series in 2006.
(Charles Wenzelberg/New York Post)

Davey Johnson looks on from the dugout during a 1987 game in Pittsburgh. In 1984, Johnson took over a Mets team that hadn't had a winning season in seven years. He led them to five consecutive 90-win seasons, including the World Series title in 1986. (Getty Images)

Stars of the 1990s and 2000s

Mets stars (left to right) Carlos Beltran, Jose Reyes, and David Wright pose in a trolley car while filming a commercial for the 2007 All-Star Game. (AP Images)

John Franco

Born: September 17, 1960
Height: 5'10" **Weight:** 170 lbs
Bats: Left **Throws:** Left

	W–L	ERA	IP	Hits	BB	K	SV
Mets (1990–2004)	48–56	3.10	702.2	685	276	592	276
Career (1984–2005)	90–87	2.89	1,245.2	1,166	495	975	424

400 Didn't Come Easy

Closer Only Second to Reach Milestone

April 16, 1999
By Brian Lewis

The achievement was as much a testament to durability as ability. John Franco had to survive the rigors of 15 years of big-league pitching on his arm, the effects of 38 years of age, and, most insidious of all, the stress of a decade of New York on his psyche.

But somehow Franco handled it all. The man whose 5'10", 185-pound frame was too small and whose mediocre fastball was too slow survived to become one of the best relievers in the history of the game. And the Met closer reminded everyone of that fact Wednesday night when he notched his historic 400th save.

After striking out the side to close out Wednesday's 4–1 win over Florida, Franco jumped in the air twice as his teammates stormed out of the dugout. As catcher Todd Pratt hoisted him in the air, Franco pointed skyward toward whatever higher power let him reach this baseball plateau and toward deceased parents Jim and Mary that watched over him while he did it.

"It was emotional," Franco admitted. "I always think about them. I wear my father's sanitation shirt for every game, I keep it close to my heart. I just wish they could've been here, at least one of them. But I know they were here in spirit. I keep them [with me] deep down inside."

Wearing a New York City Dept. of Sanitation shirt seemed fitting; with 400 saves, Franco has cleaned up a lot of messes. In his 15th year in the bigs, he trails only Lee Smith's 478 on the all-time list. And a day after his landmark save, Franco had had time to reflect on what he had done.

"It's been a long road," Franco admitted. "I remember when I signed in 1981 and I just said I wanted an opportunity to play major league ball. When I got here I wanted a chance to pitch and when I got traded to Cincinnati I got that chance. When I made it to the bigs I said I wanted to make $1 million. And after that, for 10 years, everything's just started to come into its own."

Not bad for an undersized kid from Brooklyn who was told he was too small to make it in the bigs. He was barraged with phone calls yesterday morning; including one from team president and CEO Fred Wilpon.

"My phone's been ringing a lot today. Mr. Wilpon called, my family, aunts, cousins. It's been kinda busy," Franco said, sheepishly admitting that Wilpon's call came early in the morning and was received by his answering machine.

Franco has this year and another left on his contract; Smith is squarely in his sights. Then, would even his detractors have to admit he belongs in Cooperstown?

"Absolutely. I know the word 'dominate' has stymied some voters, but the proof is in the pudding, and [in] what Johnny's done and what he continues to do," said Bobby Valentine. "And he did it in New York for 10 years. There should be an asterisk for that."

Indeed, New York is tough on any athlete, even one of their own. And Valentine thinks Franco's 400 "New York" saves should convert to something even higher in "real world" saves. After all, if Franco can make it there, he can…well, you know.

"I think it's his insides, his ability to shake off bad outings," GM Steve Phillips said of Franco. "Being a closer in New York is a little [tougher] than being a closer in Kansas City because of the reaction you get. Whether it's being a closer or a setup man or a starter. But when you're closing in New York, I don't know if it's comparable to anything in sports; and John has shown the ability to handle that."

John Franco reacts after saving a game against Atlanta in September 1998. Franco saved 38 games for the Mets that season. (Charles Wenzelberg/New York Post)

John Franco raises his cap after collecting his 400th career save against the Florida Marlins on April 14, 1999. Franco was just the second pitcher to reach 400 career saves.
(Nury Hernandez/New York Post)

John Franco's tenure as closer ended in 1999 when the Mets acquired Armando Benitez. Despite battling injuries, Franco contributed to the Mets' bullpen in a setup role during the 2000, 2001, 2003, and 2004 seasons. He was 44 years old when he pitched his final game as a Met. (Getty Images)

Todd Hundley

Born: May 27, 1969
Height: 5'11" **Weight:** 170 lbs
Bats: Both **Throws:** Right

Todd to Shea: "Hello, Honey"

Star Slugger Returns to Mets Lineup

	Games	Ave	Hits	HR	RBI	SB
Mets (1990–98)	829	.240	612	124	397	11
Career (1990–2003)	1,225	.234	883	202	599	14

July 12, 1998
By Steve Serby

Northwest Flight 524 out of Detroit from Indianapolis was descending over LaGuardia yesterday, and Todd Hundley woke from a catnap and leaned toward the window from aisle seat 4B and his face lit up the first-class cabin.

"God's country," Hundley said.

The smile stayed frozen on his boyish face because Hundley knew what was coming next.

There was Shea Stadium, empty and silent a little past noon but soon to be filled with the kind of maddening noise and love New York reserves for its beloved boys of summer. Shea has always been Hundley's field of dreams, and when you haven't played a ballgame there since last September it becomes a veritable shrine.

So Hundley—so bedraggled when the long day's journey into the hearts of his team and his town began on Northwest Flight 1724 at 7:35 AM Central Time—had become invigorated as he stared down to his left.

"Hello, honey," Hundley said.

The Comeback Kid, who had not been recognized until now, was stopped by two young boys when he stepped off the plane.

"Would you sign my hat?" one of them asked, and Hundley obliged. The other one got his baseball signed. "Welcome back to New York," a middle-aged man told him, and Hundley thanked him.

"How's your elbow?" someone else wanted to know, and Hundley, a bounce in his step all of a sudden, said: "Good, pal."

Hundley walked into the fresh air and into the arms of his pretty pregnant wife, Tiffany. Their three children, two girls and a boy, were waiting inside a van as Hundley headed back inside to baggage claim. Tiffany Hundley better than anyone knows what kind of special triumph this is for her husband, and for her.

Hundley had promised he would be back from reconstructive right elbow surgery even as he listened to the doubters talk about how fat he looked, even as he listened to the snipers who dared to talk about how tired and hung over he looked. And here he was.

Eight years a Met and damn proud of it, he broke down and cried one day when it hit him that maybe the organization had turned its back on him. And here he was.

He couldn't do much more than play Mr. Mom or collect Civil War artifacts. And here he was.

No one can be certain how he will handle the outfield, or whether he will yearn someday for his trusted tools of ignorance that now belong to Mike Piazza, or when and if he again can be one of the league's most feared sluggers and infuse blood and guts into a drowning team. But those issues could wait, at least for one day.

"It's very emotional for me," Tiffany Hundley said, "because, I mean, he's my best friend. I'm his best friend. I've been through everything with him. He was cranky to everyone but me. It's like I'm playing out there because I went through everything with him."

Now Todd Hundley gets to go through everything with Piazza, and vice versa. If Piazza is The Hollywood Matinee Idol, Hundley is The Throwback.

"I'd rather be The Throwback," Hundley said, following a Starbucks coffee break as Northwest Flight 524 sat on the runway at the Detroit Metro Airport. "It's just a game to me, it's a game of baseball that I love, that's all it is, nothing more, nothing less. Just because I'm a baseball player doesn't make me a better person than Joe Smith that's a garbage man, or Bill Smith that's a lawyer or schoolteacher or whatever."

Hundley befriended Piazza at the 1996 All-Star Game in Philadelphia, where Piazza offered Hundley a helpful batting tip.

"A lot of times, I'd get my pitch but I'd yank it foul," Hundley said. "He taught me how to keep the ball fair when you get your pitch."

Hundley was asked if he offered Piazza any subtle pointers. He smiled. "I didn't have to," he said. "Doggone, he just flat hits."

It is a measure of Hundley's character and leadership that he is now emotionally ready, if need be, to accept playing Roger Maris to Piazza's Mickey Mantle, even though he is

Todd Hundley hits a double against the Colorado Rockies at Coors Field in 1996. Hundley's 41 home runs that year set a record for most home runs by a catcher in a single season. (AP Images)

the switch-hitting homegrown product (Mantle) and Piazza is the import (Maris).

"Who's to say I can't put up better numbers in the outfield than I did as a catcher?" Hundley said. "Who's to say I can't be another All-Star outfielder, another Craig Biggio, you know?"

Hundley plans on forcing the Mets to keep him for the rest of his career.

"I'll keep putting the numbers up," Hundley vowed. "I feel I still have a lot of good years in me, especially with having the elbow done now, at age 29 instead of age 33. It'll make my career longer."

Do you think you'll hit 40 home runs again?

"Yeah," Hundley said, and smiled. "I don't think I've had a career year. I mean, obviously, yes, I've had that career year. I still think I have a better year than that left in me."

It is inevitable that some pitcher someday will complain to Hundley about Piazza. Hundley offered assurance he would move swiftly to nip any such cancer in the bud.

"Open the communication lines more," Hundley said. "Pitcher and catcher have got to be on the same page. If they're not, it's trouble. If that situation happens, hey, we gotta sit down and talk, that's all there is to it, and be honest with each other, and figure this out."

So the chemistry of the whole Met clubhouse changed the second Hundley swaggered in yesterday afternoon.

"It's more of a relaxed atmosphere that I'll bring to the team," he said. "Hey, this is a game. It's nothing more, nothing less. It's a game. Let's play the game like we did when we were kids, when we were in high school, when we were in Little League."

Hundley leaned against a wall outside the Detroit Metro Airport and recalled his first trip to the big leagues, a plane ride from Double-A Wichita to join the Davey Johnson Mets at the San Diego Marriott & Marina.

"Thinking, 'This is the only place to be,'" Hundley said.

He's back, finally, at the only place he has ever wanted to be, and the Mets are crazy if they don't want him to stay for a long, long time.

Mike Piazza

Born: September 4, 1968
Height: 6'3" **Weight:** 200 lbs
Bats: Right **Throws:** Right

	Games	Ave	Hits	HR	RBI	SB
Mets (1998–2005)	972	.296	1,028	220	655	7
Career (1992–2007)	1,912	.308	2,127	427	1,335	17

Piazza Superstar

Catcher's Big Heart Sets Example For Teammates

September 23, 2001
By Michael Morrissey

The day after rolled around, with little kids commandeering the Shea Stadium outfield for midafternoon drills with Mets personnel. The scoreboard sign read, "Welcome to Lunch Box Night."

Life moved forward, but Mike Piazza's home run still lingered in the Flushing air.

Friday night, Piazza proved once again that he is the Secretariat of major leaguers—a man with an abnormally large heart. The Mets catcher crushed a decisive two-run homer in the eighth inning to give his team a 3–2 come-from-behind victory on an evening when defeat was not an option.

"Just the noise level after he hit that home run," Robin Ventura said. "It was probably the loudest I ever heard this place."

To do what Piazza does best—hit homers, drive in runs—in a situation where a crowd of 41,235 is praying for exactly that is remarkable.

But the most remarkable aspect of the unforgettable night wasn't the victory over the hated Braves. It is how visibly moved Piazza continues to be in the wake of the Sept. 11 tragedy.

"I remember sitting down last week, just watching the news every day and just kept feeling depressed," Piazza said late Friday. "Literally depressed.

"But I was thinking, 'You know what? I have to do something, and it might as well be something productive.' And obviously people in the whole country are getting back to work."

The Mets went back to work at Shea for the first time since a terrorist attack left the entire nation shaken. The players continued to don the hats of those who had fallen in the World Trade Center attack, and Piazza was sporting a helmet with "NYPD" glued on behind the plate.

During the emotional pregame ceremonies that featured Diana Ross and Marc Anthony, Piazza (like many) fought his overflowing emotions. Some media reports indicated he cried; others left the description at a quivering upper lip.

Whatever the case, the transplanted New Yorker, now living in Gramercy Park not far from the WTC, made an error that cost his team a run early. He failed to snag a one-hop relay throw in the fourth, allowing Chipper Jones to score the first Atlanta run.

Piazza, who strikes even casual baseball observers as a more human, more approachable superstar, atoned later in the game.

With the Mets down 2–1 with one out and one on in the eighth, Piazza turned on an 0–1 pitch from Braves right-hander Steve Karsay. It was a little low and a little outside, but Piazza deposited it 420 feet away into a camera stand just left of center field.

The fastball was either 96 or 94 miles per hour, depending on the radar gun.

"As an athlete, you have a way of not putting that pressure on yourself because you're up there and they're throwing the ball 97 miles per hour," Piazza said. "I had a way to stay relaxed. I felt relaxed.

"That was definitely in the back of our minds."

With the city and the nation hurting as badly as it is, Piazza is careful not to identify himself as anything more than a diversion. He and his teammates continue to praise the city's firemen, policemen, EMTs and others, many of whom were watching him for their cue last night.

"I just think it's great the bravery they continue to show," he said. "God forbid, if that situation were to reoccur tomorrow, they all would've done what they did."

Mike Piazza wears a New York Police Department cap during the Mets' September 17, 2001, game against the Pittsburgh Pirates in Pittsburgh. The game was the Mets' first since the September 11, 2001, terrorist attacks. (Francis Specker/New York Post)

Above: Mike Piazza approaches Roger Clemens on the pitcher's mound after Clemens threw Piazza's broken bat at Piazza as the Mets catcher ran to first base during the first inning of Game 2 of the 2000 World Series. Home plate umpire Charlie Reliford tries to keep peace between the two superstars. (Getty Images)

Right: Mike Piazza hit 220 home runs for the Mets over eight seasons. The catcher led the team in home runs and RBIs when the Mets advanced to the 1999 National League Championship Series and 2000 World Series. (Getty Images)

Edgardo Alfonzo

Born: August 11, 1973
Height: 5'11"   **Weight:** 185 lbs
Bats: Right   **Throws:** Right

	Games	Ave	Hits	HR	RBI	SB
Mets (1995–2002)	1,086	.292	1,136	120	538	45
Career (1995–2006)	1,506	.284	1,532	146	744	53

Speak Softly and Carry a Big Stick
Humble Fonzie Lets Potent Bat Do The Talking

October 12, 1999
By Dan Martin

Not many players can develop a knack for hitting huge home runs in October, while playing in New York, and still remain virtually anonymous to those outside the Big Apple. But that's what Edgardo Alfonzo is doing.

In the Mets' first most important game since 1988, the 25-year-old blasted a home run to lead the Mets to a 5–0 win over the Reds. Alfonzo's hit helped his team reach the playoffs for the first time in 11 years. He then slammed a pair of homers, including a game-winning grand slam to lead the Mets over Arizona in the first game of the NLDS.

"He's been doing this for us all year," Robin Ventura said. "It's just now he's been doing it more. He's become someone we can really count on in big spots."

With this string of huge performances, including Alfonzo's solo home run in the clinching win over the Diamondbacks, he seems to be making a run at becoming the new "Mr. October."

But don't expect the mild-mannered Venezuelan to make too many bold Reggie Jackson–like proclamations any time soon. He may be the straw that stirs the Mets, but Alfonzo's lack of renown doesn't bother him and comes as no surprise to his manager—despite the fact that he has become the best second baseman this side of Cleveland's Roberto Alomar.

"He talks with his bat," Bobby Valentine said. "He's a young player yet and he didn't burst on the scene and start playing every day. So people put a tag on him with limitations. He's proving those people wrong."

Those people are not in the Mets organization. But even general manager Steve Phillips couldn't have expected what he has gotten.

"I knew Edgardo as an 18-year-old," said Phillips, who

was the Mets' Director of Minor League Personnel while Alfonzo made his way up the system. "He was a heady player even then, but you never know for sure how they'll perform in big games. Obviously, he's come through."

That is quite an understatement. A fitting way to describe one of baseball's most understated players. After a season in which Alfonzo hit .304 with 27 home runs and 108 RBIs, all while playing a practically flawless second base, there is no telling how hot he could be. If Alfonzo was so inclined, he could be selling his name all over the city—maybe even on a candy bar. Don't hold your breath. He craves attention the way most of us crave wisdom teeth.

"Edgardo is one of the classiest people I have ever met," said ex–major leaguer Rick Waits, one of the Mets pitching instructors. "He's stayed so down to earth. That's what makes him different."

Opposing pitchers wish that was all that made Alfonzo unique. Waits, however, knows there is much more that sets him apart. He served as the pitching coach with Alfonzo's Venezuelan winter league team, Magallenes, from 1996–98 and has seen the second baseman do just about anything.

"He's such a special player. I've seen him have so many clutch hits down there, but that's not all," Waits said. "He has always done the right thing. He always gets hits when we've needed them. He could probably play the outfield, too. The home runs, though, that's new."

They have even caught Alfonzo a little off guard.

"I'm a little surprised by all the home runs," Alfonzo said. "I don't really do anything different [in critical situations]. I try to keep the same approach."

And although Alfonzo is still a young player, he realizes the finality of the postseason. Last year's Mets collapse taught him to take nothing for granted.

"You've got to perform at all times," Alfonzo said. "Especially at the end of the season. It's good that I've done that."

Since the dramatic shots are there, why not take advantage of them?

"I don't want people to think that I want any kind of recognition," Alfonzo said. "I'm not looking to do anything but win baseball games and help my team win."

He has done that, especially lately. And if Alfonzo doesn't watch out, he might get that candy bar, after all.

Edgardo Alfonzo throws out a St. Louis Cardinals runner at first base during an April 2002 game at Shea Stadium. After moving from third base to second at the beginning of the 1999 season, Alfonzo won the Silver Slugger award in 1999 and was an All-Star in 2000. (Charles Wenzelberg/New York Post)

Carlos Delgado

Born: June 25, 1972
Height: 6'3" **Weight:** 215 lbs
Bats: Left **Throws:** Right

	Games	Ave	Hits	HR	RBI	SB
Mets (2006-09)	468	.267	468	104	339	5
Career (1993-2009)	2,035	.280	2,038	473	1,512	14

Great First Impression
Delgado Makes Postseason Splash with Mets

October 5, 2006
By Kevin Kernan

Up until yesterday, Carlos Delgado never participated in postseason baseball. Now you can call him "Mr. October," at least for one night.

Delgado went into yesterday's NL Division Series opener having played 1,711 major league games without making it to the playoffs, the longest streak of any active player.

At the age of 34, he is a postseason rookie.

In one day, that all changed.

Delgado turned into Reggie Jackson and Derek Jeter all at once as he led the Mets to a pulsating 6–5 win over the Dodgers at Shea Stadium in Game 1 of the NLDS.

Delgado slugged a mammoth solo home run off Derek Lowe to get the Mets' offense started in the fourth inning, tying the game 1–1. He lined a run-scoring single to left-center in the seventh to put the Mets ahead 5–4, after the Dodgers came back from a 4–1 deficit to tie the game.

The lefty slugger drilled four hits in five at-bats with two RBIs and two runs scored, including an impressive slide at home plate that Jeter would have been proud to pull off.

"I hope it gets better," Delgado said of his postseason magic.

Move over Reggie, if it does.

The Mets' clubhouse was thrilled with the win and thrilled with Delgado.

"You have so much respect for him as a teammate, but he is one of the best individuals off the field that I've ever played with," Paul Lo Duca said. "To have this kind of game to start his postseason career is unbelievable—and it couldn't happen to a better person."

Delgado had some home run help; Cliff Floyd also crushed a solo homer in the fourth.

The biggest difference between the Mets and Dodgers is power. The Mets have it, the Dodgers don't. It's the difference between the laid-back West Coast and the gritty, let's-make-it-through-the-day-any-way-we-can East Coast.

The Dodgers were last in home runs in the National League with 153. The Mets hit 200. Forty-seven more times than the Dodgers they rounded the bases on a home run.

The Big Fly lives here.

Delgado hit 38 of them during the regular season and has 407 in his career. Now he has one postseason home run.

Last week, discussing the upcoming opportunity of playing his first postseason, Delgado said, "I think I'll be able to handle it, but I don't know. I'm a rookie at this."

He's not a rookie anymore.

Delgado's blast was a wakeup call for the Mets' offense. It came on a 2–1 sinking fastball from Derek Lowe. Delgado lifted a bomb to center that landed on the roof of the TV tower, an estimated 470 feet from home plate. When the center-field camera is pointing straight up, you know you got it all.

It was a statement home run, majestic, just what the Mets needed. It made all the pitching calf problems go away—for the moment.

The seventh-inning single was more important because the Mets had given up a late lead. They needed another monster hit, and Delgado stepped up and delivered against Brad Penny.

Delgado earned his playoff stripes. He is ready to carry the Mets this October.

"I had butterflies in my stomach the first couple of innings," Delgado said.

The trick is to get those butterflies in flying formation. Delgado said he did just that.

"I was able to control my emotions," he said.

David Wright was there at home plate to congratulate Delgado after the home run.

"He definitely did not control his emotions," countered Wright, whose seventh-inning double knocked in what turned out to be the winning run. "He almost took my arm off, hitting my hand on the home run."

When Delgado was announced as the player of the game, the crowd of 56,979 gave him one last huge cheer. In his first postseason game, after waiting a baseball lifetime to play in October, Delgado had won over a city.

Carlos Delgado poses on the Shea Stadium field in November 2005 after the Mets acquired Delgado from the Florida Marlins. The Puerto Rican first baseman hit 38 home runs and drove in 114 runs for the 2006 National League East champion Mets. (Charles Wenzelberg/New York Post)

David Wright

Born: December 20, 1982
Height: 6'0"   **Weight:** 210 lbs
Bats: Right   **Throws:** Right

	Games	Ave	Hits	HR	RBI	SB
Mets (2004–)	1,004	.305	1,149	169	664	138
Career (2004–)	1,004	.305	1,149	169	664	138

**Statistics through 2010

Can Do No Wrong   David Always Makes Wright Move

August 23, 2007
By Kevin Kernan

This was another New York dream day for David Wright.

At 11:30 he showed up in Times Square at a promotion for Vitaminwater, where a panel of fans played a guessing game with his life. The energy drink company even has a website called DavidWrightorWrong.com.

When was his first kiss? What was his first job? What was the name of his high school? Was he the class vice president? What TV show would he like to be on: *American Idol, Dancing with the Stars* or *Deal or No Deal?*

Wright spent an hour and a half at the ESPN Zone interacting with his fans and helping to raise money for the David Wright Foundation, and loved every minute of it. He then went to work at Shea Stadium where the Mets took on Jake Peavy and the Padres.

Though every night is Game 7 for the Yankees, Wright's Mets are starting to pull away from the pack in the downtrodden NL East. They went into last night's game five games ahead of the Phillies, who will have to live the next two weeks without ace Cole Hamels, and six games ahead of the Braves.

Wright and the Mets are finding their groove, although Peavy figured to be a difficult test.

The Mets have scored five or more runs in nine straight games, tying the franchise record set in 1990 and matched in 2002 and 2006. With Wright batting third and Carlos Beltran fourth, the offense is coming together.

Beltran is hitting like the postseason-Astros Carlos Beltran, Jose Reyes is running and scoring runs at a frenetic pace, and Wright continues to do his thing. He is a perfect mix of power and speed.

Wright went into last night hitting .339 over the last 75 games. In only 14 of those has he not managed a hit. Over his last 21 games, Wright is batting .410. Wright is tied for eighth in the NL with 25 stolen bases. Over the last 11 games Wright has three home runs and 11 games. He has 22 home runs, three less than team-leader Beltran, and he owns 79 RBIs, one less that Beltran. Wright leads the club with 30 doubles and in total bases with 242.

At the age of 24, Wright once again is having a tremendous season, batting .310.

All this goes to show that no matter what goes wrong for the Mets, they will always have Wright. The third baseman is all about consistency.

Though Beltran runs hot and cold, and no one gets hotter than Beltran, Wright has been putting together solid at-bats all season. He remains a favorite of the fans with his electric smile and electric bat. That was evident yesterday as the Times Square fans got a look into David's world.

For the record, his first kiss came at the age of 13. His first job was an assistant at a batting cage. And yes, when he was at Hickory High he was class vice president. Of the three TV shows mentioned, he would love to appear on *Deal or No Deal.*

Wright knows how to make a deal. He signed a new deal with the Mets for $55 million in the offseason and was wise enough to take stock options from Vitaminwater when he started promoting the company years ago.

Wright laughed and smiled through the entire session with the fans.

"This is why I love playing in New York," he said. "The fans really care about you and know so much about you as a player and a person."

Even though Wright has been around for four seasons now, there are times he seems too good to be true, but Wright wants to be a complete player in many ways. That's why he loves to steal bases and show power. Five more stolen bases and eight more home runs and Wright will become the Mets' first 30-30 player since Howard Johnson in 1991.

"You want to be known as a complete player," Wright said. "You don't want to be just a power guy or a speed guy, you want to do both."

Speed or power, Wright can't go wrong.

David Wright poses during spring training in 2010. The Mets' supplemental first-round pick in the 2001 draft, Wright batted over .300 in each of his first five full seasons and has been named to five All-Star teams. (Getty Images)

Carlos Beltran

Born: April 24, 1977
Height: 6'1"   **Weight:** 215 lbs
Bats: Both   **Throws:** Right

October Legend's 'Tran-Tastic Again
Beltran Excels in the Postseason

	Games	Ave	Hits	HR	RBI	SB
**Mets (2005–2011)	741	.279	776	134	493	97
Career (1998–)	1,626	.282	1,761	280	1,062	289

**Statistics through 2010

October 13, 2006
By Mike Vaccaro

The place was church-still, odd for an October night, odder still given the circumstances: scoreless game, bottom of the sixth, one of those pitchers' duels that generally gets the poets' motors revving. Just not Shea Stadium. Just not now. Maybe it was the chill in the air. Maybe it was the residue of a long Wednesday. Whatever.

The Mets always believed Carlos Beltran was the kind of player who could turn a picture like that upside down, who could wave a bat like a magic wand and bring magic to a night such as this one. Jeff Weaver had him down 0–2. Beltran fought back to 2–2.

Weaver came with a fastball. Beltran swung.

And by the time it tumbled back to earth, by the time it smacked against the HIP sign in right-center field 430 feet away, suddenly the place wasn't so quiet anymore. Suddenly the night wasn't so still.

And suddenly the game wasn't tied anymore either. It was 2–0, on the way to a 1–0 lead for the Mets in this best-of-seven National League Championship Series.

This was how he'd gotten here in the first place, if you think about it.

Two years ago, Beltran entered October as one of baseball's great secrets, a sparkling flash of a player who'd spent most of his career tucked away in Kansas City, well out of the way of oncoming fame and fortune.

Then, by manner of introduction, he had one of the great postseasons of all time.

He hit four home runs against the Braves in a five-game Division Series.

He hit four more against the Cardinals in the seven-game NLCS.

He'd batted .455 against the Braves, and .417 against the Cards, and it seemed that every time you flicked on the television, he was trotting around the basepaths.

He became a must-have player across those 12 games in 2004, the kind of player you not only build a team around, but a franchise.

The Mets paid him $119 million to be that franchise-type player that they hadn't had since Mike Piazza had started to act his age.

He came here and he was dreadful for a full season; he was booed, he was berated.

He'd been hurt most of that first season but nobody really wanted to hear about that, not as long as his name was in the lineup every day. In September, as the season grew short and the Shea crowds sparse, he found his face installed in a most-unpleasant-rogues gallery of Mets images, faces like Robbie Alomar and Mo Vaughn and the like, players who had once been great, then forgot all about how to be great once they got to Shea Stadium.

Beltran was traveling a similar path, if not the same road.

Except from the start of this 2006 season, Beltran seemed more comfortable in almost every way: in his uniform, in his clubhouse, and in his skin. Maybe Carlos Delgado's arrival had something to do with that. Maybe a healthier body and healthier outlook did.

He hit a homer in St. Louis early in the season. He had maybe his signature moment of the season against the Cards at Shea in late August, a bottom-of-the-ninth, walkoff homer that electrified the place, gave it an October timbre even in the doggiest of the dog days.

And there he was last night, one more time, the ballgame mired in a scoreless tie, the Mets having spent 5⅔ innings entranced by Jeff Weaver, the ballpark quiet, a nervous wreck, waiting for someone in home whites to seize the night, and the moment, by the throat.

Finding that elusive someone hitting third in the order, stepping up to the plate after Paul Lo Duca snuck a two-out single—only the Mets' second hit of the night—then falling behind 0-and-2, then working his way back into a count, then looking for a fastball.

And getting the fastball.

And then trying to hit it clear over the night. Beltran had been quiet in the first-round win over the Dodgers, and revealed a few days ago that he has an abdominal tear, and maybe that was the reason and maybe it wasn't.

Maybe he was just waiting to see those Cardinals uniforms, the ones that seem to kick his game into an extra gear.

Carlos Beltran rounds the bases after hitting a solo home run against the Arizona Diamondbacks in June 2005. Signed as a free agent before the 2005 season, Beltran has been named an All-Star five times and won three Gold Gloves since joining the Mets. (Charles Wenzelberg/New York Post)

Johan Santana

Born: March 13, 1979
Height: 6'0" **Weight:** 195 lbs
Bats: Left **Throws:** Left

	W-L	ERA	IP	Hits	BB	K	CG
**Mets (2008-)	40-25	2.85	600	541	164	496	7
Career (2000-)	133-69	3.10	1908.2	1609	528	1877	13

**Statistics through 2010

Johan's Luck Typical of Ace
Wins Hard to Come by Against League's Best

July 6, 2008
By Mike Vaccaro

The look is always the same, one of professional acceptance.

Sometimes, a whisper of frustration seeps through, sometimes more.

Last Saturday, after a 3–2 loss to the Yankees, Johan Santana had allowed that all he can do is throw the ball, do his job. He has to trust that the other men on the Mets will do theirs eventually, too.

It's a familiar complaint by fine pitchers. Once, after losing a pitcher's duel to Tim Wakefield in the 2003 American League Championship Series, Mike Mussina grew testy at questioners and mused, "All I can worry about is 60 feet, six inches." Meaning, sometimes you pitch lousy and get hammered.

But more often, if you're good enough, you pitch terrific and lose.

That's one of the great hidden arithmetical truths in baseball: the better a pitcher you are, the harder it sometimes is to win games. The mathematics of a pitching rotation dictates that more often than not, an ace collides with another ace.

It's a reality Santana has faced time after time this year, matching up twice with Tim Hudson (two losses), twice with Andy Pettitte (a win and a loss), twice with Dan Haren (two no-decisions), and once with Cole Hamels (a win).

There have been meetings with Ben Sheets (loss), John Lackey (loss), and Felix Hernandez (loss).

"I have to do my job," he said Friday night after picking up a no-decision in the Mets' 3–2 loss to the Phillies, his record sticking at 7–7, the Mets' record in his starts falling to a remarkable 9–9, including 0–6 in the last six, "and have faith that everything else will take care of itself." If you are a Mets fan and it seems you can't shake an unending sense of déjà vu watching Santana this year, it is understandable. Because if you are old enough to have followed the career of Tom Seaver, you know what it's like when your sure thing is no sure thing, even if he's as close to a sure thing as sure things can be.

Seaver, after all, did win 311 games, and did win 198 with the Mets, and did win three Cy Young Awards, and did pile up 98 percent of the vote in his first year of Cooperstown consideration.

But if there are two prevailing memories for Mets fans of a certain age, it is this:

Seaver always drawing Bob Gibson, or Juan Marichal, or Steve Carlton, or Ferguson Jenkins, or Phil Niekro. And Seaver always embroiled in a game that ended 1–0, 2–0, or 2–1.

That first one really is the product of the mind doing tricks on you, because just as often Seaver found himself paired with Reggie Cleveland or Carl Morton or Ray Burris or Clay Kirby (just as Santana found himself matched with J.A. Happ Friday night). But the second is actually quite true.

Seaver started 395 games for the Mets. In 143 of them—more than 36 percent—the Mets scored two or fewer runs for him. More than one out of every three times Seaver took the mound as a Met, he knew he was going to have to be perfect, or damn near close, if he wanted to have a shot at winning.

And in 228 of those games—58 percent of them—the Mets actually did win. He didn't always get credit for the win, but you'd better believe he gets credit for making those wins possible.

On his own record, Seaver won six 1–0 games as a Met (and, tellingly, lost nine 1–0). He won five games 2–0 (and lost eight). But what's really remarkable is his record in 2–1 games, the kind that really test the mettle of an ace—and, not incidentally, the kind of score the Mets would have been glad to have won by Friday, when they took a 2–0 lead into the sixth—because those are nights when you don't have shut-down, shutout stuff but you find a way to make due with the runs you get.

In those games, and there were 38 of them in which Seaver got credit for a decision in his 11½ years with the Mets, Seaver was 23–15.

More often than not, he was going to find a way. Your memory isn't playing tricks on you.

Johan Santana grips the baseball during spring training in 2008. Although he has missed some time due to injuries, Santana has posted a 40–25 mark and 2.85 earned run average since joining the Mets. (Getty Images)

Jose Reyes

Born: March 13, 1979
Height: 6'0" **Weight:** 195 lbs
Bats: Left **Throws:** Left

	Games	Ave	Hits	HR	RBI	SB
**Mets (2003-)	924	.286	1,119	74	379	331
Career (2003-)	924	.286	1,119	74	379	331

**Statistics through 2010

Dominican Dream Realized

Shortstop Showed Promise from a Young Age

July 3, 2011
By Rafael Fellito Ortiz & Ginger Adams Otis

Thirty years ago, under the blazing Dominican sun, a poor young farmer, preparing to marry his childhood sweetheart, hacked at the stubborn plants around him and made an impassioned plea to God.

"There I was, pulling up [sugarcane] stumps, with my fingers all destroyed, and one day I just threw the machete into the sugarcane. I just threw it," the man says. "And I said, 'God, the day I marry Rosa, please give me a baseball-player son.'"

Boy, did God deliver!

That farmer's first child, a skinny, hyperactive boy who from the cradle was "afanoso," or driven, is Jose Reyes.

The Mets superstar is one of the most exciting stories in the game right now. The 28-year-old is in the middle of a season for the ages, in which entering yesterday's game his .352 batting average and 15 triples led the Major Leagues—he's second in hits and stolen bases—and the statistics he's accumulated in his first 1,000 games are being compared to those of the legendary Ty Cobb.

The MVP-type numbers come at the perfect time for Reyes, who's bouncing back from two injury-marred seasons and who could command a long-term, $160 million contract when he becomes a free agent in October. But Reyes suffered a bit of a scare yesterday when he felt tightness in his left hamstring and exited the Mets' 5–2 loss after two innings. He'll undergo an MRI today.

For always-pessimistic Mets fans, the sizzling season thus far has the feel of a bravura encore; the beleaguered Wilpon family ownership may not be able—or willing—to keep the star whose exuberant style of play has given the team its brightest highlight over the past 10 years.

Unlike his nervous fan base, Reyes seems immune to the anxieties of an uncertain future. He continues to flash his wide grin and after every hit pump the "claw" in the air—a gesture he picked up from fellow Dominican shortstop Miguel Tejada.

"I want to be here. It's too soon to say, so for now I just want to continue to play and continue to play good," he told The Post Friday. "I love the fans. They've always been good to me, always supported me. I thank them for it."

Reyes' meteoric rise surpasses every expectation his humble dad, Jose Manuel Reyes, who hails from "a tiny house in the hills with a palm-leaf roof," had for his son.

Jose Manuel eventually left his small farm to work in a factory making bathroom accessories, and later opened a bodega in front of the humble, one-bedroom home that he, wife Rosa, son Jose, and daughter Miosotis shared in Palmar Arriba, a small suburb of Villa Gonzalez, an agricultural area of 30,000 residents.

Rail thin and lightning quick, young Reyes was a standout even as a pre-teen playing for his dad's laid-back softball team.

"I brought him to play one day for the factory team, and a friend saw him in action and said to me, 'If you want to get something out of this kid, then get him out of the countryside,'" says Jose Manuel, 54.

Dad was willing, but Jose, shy and in no hurry to leave home—his mother's rice and beans is still his favorite dish—didn't want to join the Felix de Leon League for kids his age. It was located 20 minutes away in Santiago, the second-largest city in the Dominican Republic.

"At first I'd just take him on Saturdays, but he was afraid and told me he'd never go to Santiago. Then, bit by bit, as he saw the other kids practicing and playing, he'd go join in. Then he started going alone, and finally he'd travel with them to towns farther away for tournaments," says Jose Manuel.

From the start, young Jose kept "giving them surprises" with his talent, says the proud papi.

"He has always had a natural ability to get to third base on any decent hit, it's just an instinctive thing for him," he says.

In fact, the only hitter in history with more triples and stolen bases in his first 1,000 games is Hall-of-Famer Cobb.

But it's more than stats for the fans, who adore Jose's quirky tics—like wagging his tongue back and forth as he blurs around the bases, or doing his dugout dance after a home run.

For many years he did the popular "Professor Reyes" series, a Spanish lesson that played on the big screen at Shea Stadium and then Citi Field between innings.

As beloved as Reyes is in New York, it's nothing compared to how he's viewed in the Dominican Republic.

"I've known Jose since our childhood, since we were five years old, and he's an excellent person. He's a millionaire, but he's the same guy. He comes here, he plays with us, he hangs out just like he always did," says longtime buddy Héctor Alvarez.

The whole town "vibrates" when Reyes comes up to bat or gets on base, Alvarez says. Everyone's glued to the TV set to catch the inevitable moment when the twitchy Reyes takes off for another steal.

"It's with one voice that everyone screams, 'Jose Reyes!'" says Alvarez. "He's a real icon here."

Nowadays, kids like Osiris Tatis, 11, who wants to be a shortstop like his idol, play el béisbol on a gleaming diamond carved from a rock-strewn lot.

It's the House that Jose Reyes built.

Reyes, who inked a four-year, $23.25 million contract with the Mets in 2007, is a millionaire many times over.

But he shares liberally with family and friends and has funneled hundreds of thousands of dollars into converting the weed-choked empty lot where he used to play into the modest but state-of-the-art stadium.

He's also helped create a league to foster young talent in his hometown and other cities around the Dominican Republic.

He pays the salaries of the young coaches who work at Jose Reyes Field, provides exercise machines, bats, balls, gloves, and other equipment, and has poured hundreds of thousands of dollars into the creation of a local league that fosters new talent in Santiago and around the country.

"This field is a blessing for us," says Osiris, taking a break Thursday from a late-night game. "When Jose comes, he plays with us. He brings us equipment and things we need from the United States."

When Reyes was a boy, however, none of that existed.

He and his friends scrounged around to find old milk cartons or other bits of cardboard to fashion baseball mitts. They played on whatever semiclear surface they could find. Bats and balls were scarce.

But Reyes never let the poverty around him get him down, says his mother, Rosa, who will be in New York this week to visit her son.

"He liked to swim in the nearby river, play in the mango fields, ride his bike. He was always very active," says Rosa, from inside the two-story home that her son had built for her when he was 16 and got a $22,000 signing bonus from the Mets.

He had it constructed it atop the one-bedroom home where he grew up—about 200 yards from the renovated Jose Reyes Field.

Reyes was called up to the majors in June 2003, the day before his 20th birthday.

In 2007, he and his future wife, Katherine, 29—a friend in 2003 set him up on a date with the Dominican knockout in New York—moved from their two-bedroom apartment in Bayside, Queens.

The couple took daughters Katherine, 6, and Ashley, 5—they've since added Joselyn, 2—to Manhasset, LI, to the six-bedroom, 4½-bathroom colonial mansion Reyes bought for $3.25 million.

He kept the purchase a secret from his parents until they arrived for the baseball season. When he drove them in from the airport and pulled his car into the driveway, Rosa began to cry, and Jose Manuel was speechless.

Jose Reyes is all smiles in the Mets dugout during the 2011 season. The four-time All-Star has led the National League in stolen bases three times and triples three times. (AP Images)

In 2008 Reyes married his longtime girlfriend in a no-frills ceremony at City Hall. For his honeymoon, he returned the next night to Shea Stadium to knock out a home run, two doubles, and a single in a game the Mets eventually lost. Torn hamstrings and a hyperactive thyroid hobbled Reyes during parts of 2009 and 2010, but he's been back in form this season.

Reyes, who hasn't cut his dreadlocks since 2008, is open about his desire to finish his career in the city he loves—but he's also refused to negotiate a new contract with the Mets until the end of the season, saying it's a distraction.

"He loves New York, the diversity, the fans who always treat him great, and the energy of the city—he's a small-town guy but that energy feeds him," says his agent, Chris Lieble, who is also godfather to Reyes' two oldest daughters.

Reyes isn't anticipating having to pull his children out of their schools or give up his favorite Manhattan hangouts, like STK in the Meatpacking District or Tao, Lieble says.

"He's said all along that he just wants to help the Mets win," the agent says. "He'd also love to win the World Series—he's always said that's his Number 1 goal."

Reyes, playing right now at the peak of his ability, brims with confidence at the plate.

"I think I'm going to get on base every time. This is the best I've felt in years," he says.

Franchise Builders

Mets owner Joan Payson and manager Casey Stengel share a laugh before the 1965 season opener at Shea Stadium. Payson was the Mets' founding owner and Stengel the franchise's first manager. (Jacobellis/New York Post)

From the National League awarding an expansion team to New York in response to the threat of a proposed third major league to the team's management shakeup prior to the 2011 season, the Mets' ownership and management have often provided storylines as compelling as those of the players on the field.

After the Giants and Dodgers left New York for California after the 1957 season, New York mayor Robert Wagner asked prominent attorney William Shea to chair a committee to return the National League to New York. After efforts to lure an existing team to move proved unsuccessful and the National League showed no interest in expanding, Shea and former Dodgers executive Branch Rickey announced the formation of a third major league, the Continental League. Ownership groups were formed in five cities: New York, Houston, Minneapolis–St. Paul, Denver, and Toronto.

Mets majority owner Joan Payson ceremonially taps a bat onto a bottle of champagne held by board chairman M. Donald Grant as the franchise officially announced the expansion team's name in May 1961. Pictured from left are Mets president George Weiss, National League president Warren Giles, baseball commissioner Ford Frick, Payson, and Grant. (AP Images)

The threat of a third major league forced the American League and National League to respond, which they did as each league expanded by two teams in the early 1960s—the American League adding teams in Washington, D.C. (to replace the Senators, who had relocated to Minneapolis–St. Paul) and Los Angeles and the National League awarding franchises to Houston and New York.

New York's franchise was awarded to the city's Continental League ownership group, headed by Joan Whitney Payson, a wealthy heiress and former minority owner of the New York Giants who opposed the move to California and subsequently sold her shares in the team. Also part of the ownership group of the team that became the Mets was M. Donald Grant, the only other Giants director who opposed the move. Mrs. Payson was a pioneer in American sports, the first woman to attain majority control of a major franchise by purchasing it rather than inheriting it. She served as the team's president from 1968 until her death in 1975.

When the Mets were formed, George Weiss was brought in to serve as the team's first president and general manager. As the general manager of the Yankees from 1947 to 1960, Weiss assembled seven World Series championship teams. Weiss's Mets teams were less successful, finishing last in the National League four times in five seasons. But the executive did help fill the Polo Grounds and Shea Stadium by placing Mets uniforms on well-known figures as Casey Stengel, Yogi Berra, Gil Hodges, Richie Ashburn, Warren Spahn, and Duke Snider. Weiss also acquired young pitchers Tom Seaver and Tug McGraw, who would prove to be key members of the 1969 World Series team.

Johnny Murphy, a former major league relief pitcher and Red Sox executive, was named Mets general manager in 1967. Murphy played a key role in acquiring manager Gil Hodges from the Washington Senators and he assembled the roster of the 1969 "Miracle Mets" World Series team. Sadly, Murphy suffered a heart attack and passed away in January 1970 at age 61, just a few months after the World Series.

Following Mrs. Payson's death in 1975, her husband, Charles Payson, daughter, Lorinda de Roulet, and minority owner M. Donald Grant assumed

Bill Shea throws out the first ball at the opening game at Shea Stadium on April 17, 1964. A prominent attorney, Shea paved the way for an expansion team to be awarded to New York, and the Mets' new ballpark was named in his honor. **(AP Images)**

operations of the club. The franchise struggled on the field, beginning a stretch of seven consecutive losing seasons in 1977. Grant is widely blamed for the contentious contract negotiations with Tom Seaver that ultimately led to his trade to the Cincinnati Reds.

In 1980, the Payson family sold controlling interest in the Mets to the publishing company Doubleday & Co., headed by Nelson Doubleday. Also part of the ownership group was Fred Wilpon, president of Sterling Equities, Inc. Wilpon served as team president from 1980 to 2002. After Bertelsmann AG purchased Doubleday & Co. in 1986, Doubleday and Wilpon purchased the Mets for $80 million. In 2002, the Wilpon family bought out Nelson Doubleday's share to become the majority owner of the Mets.

After Doubleday and Wilpon purchased the Mets in 1980, one of their first moves was to hire Frank Cashen as the team's general manager. The longtime executive had been part of putting together the Baltimore Orioles teams that won the 1966 and 1970 World Series. Cashen went to work in revamping the Mets' farm system. He drafted Dwight Gooden and Darryl Strawberry, who developed into the best hitter and pitcher in franchise history, respectively. Cashen traded for Keith Hernandez, Gary Carter, and Ron

Darling. And Davey Johnson was hired to manage the Mets before the 1984 season. The sum of these parts was the 1986 Mets World Series championship team.

Steve Phillips joined the Mets front office in 1990 and ascended to the general manager's chair in 1997. Under Phillips' watch, the Mets acquired David Wright and Jose Reyes and obtained several key veterans who played roles on the 2000 World Series team, including Mike Piazza, Robin Ventura, and Al Leiter. Phillips was let go in June 2003 and moved on to a broadcasting career with ESPN. In 2009, ESPN let Phillips go after it was revealed that he had an affair with an ESPN production assistant.

Omar Minaya grew up just minutes from Shea Stadium in Queens. After a short playing career and a stint in the Texas Rangers' front office, Minaya joined the Mets in the mid-1990s. Eventually he became Phillips' assistant general manager before leaving the Mets in 2002 to become general manager of the Montreal Expos. Fred Wilpon lured Minaya back to New York to become the Mets general manager after the 2004 season. In his first off-season, Minaya added pitcher Pedro Martinez and outfielder Carlos Beltran and the team improved by 12 games to 83 wins and playoff contention in

Frank Cashen introduces Davey Johnson as the Mets' new manager during an October 1983 press conference. Cashen took over a struggling franchise in 1980 and assembled a team that won the World Series in 1986. (AP Images)

Mets general manager Johnny Murphy and manager Gil Hodges meet on the field during spring training in 1969. Murphy assembled the 1969 World Series championship team. (Getty Images)

2005. Before the 2006 season, Minaya added a group of veterans that included closer Billy Wagner and first baseman Carlos Delgado. The Mets tied the Yankees for the best regular-season record in baseball and advanced to within one win of the World Series.

In January 2008, Minaya acquired ace pitcher Johan Santana from Minnesota for four prospects. Minaya and Mets manager Jerry Manuel were let go after the 2010 season. The Mets hired former Oakland Athletics executive Sandy Alderson as general manager before the 2011 season. Also, following revelations that the Wilpon family and the Mets' finances were involved in the Bernard Madoff Ponzi scheme, Fred Wilpon agreed to sell a minority share of the Mets to David Einhorn, the president of the hedge fund Greenlight Capital in May 2011.

Covered in champagne, general manager Steve Phillips talks to the Media after the Mets defeated the St. Louis Cardinals in the 2000 National League Championship series to earn the franchise's fourth trip to the World Series. (AP Images)

Omar Minaya talks to the media in the Mets dugout prior to a May 2010 game. In five-plus years as general manager, Minaya put together a 2006 team that finished tied for the best record in baseball and acquired ace Johan Santana from the Minnesota Twins. (Charles Wenzelberg/New York Post)

Mets owners Nelson Doubleday (left) and Fred Wilpon (right) pose with Mike Piazza during an October 1998 press conference where it was announced that Piazza had re-signed with the Mets. (Charles Wenzelberg/New York Post)

Greatest Games of the 1960s, '70s, and '80s

Gary Carter leads the cheers after the Mets took a 1986 World Series game from the Boston Red Sox. (Getty Images)

	123	456	789	R H E
New York Yankees	010	100	001	3 10 2
New York Mets	000	012	001	4 7 0

Mets Handed Stengel a Win to Remember

EXPANSION TEAM TOPS BOMBERS IN EXHIBITION BY LEONARD SHECTER

When Casey Stengel walked into the special press room here last night he was wearing a blue serge suit, slicked back hair, and a cat-that-ate-the-canary expression.

The hard-nosed reporters, radio and TV men present, who had been guzzling Mrs. C. S. Payson's booze and gobbling her caviar and hors d'oeuvres; broke into applause. It was the most heartwarming exhibition of emotion since Shirley Temple declared her undying love for Steppin' Fetchit.

Stengel raised his large hands and waved them like a Philharmonic conductor, deprecating applause and asking for silence. "It shows you," he said, "how easy this business is."

It was the climax of a triumphant day, probably there hasn't been one like it since the Allies marched into Paris. For it was the day in which the new New York team beat the old New York team and the way it happened couldn't have been more thrilling. It was good for the Mets, it was good for baseball. It may have even been good for the Yankees.

The score was 4–3 and the Mets won it in the ninth after failing to hold a 3–2 lead in the ninth because their infield play is what you'd expect of a new baseball team. (Still, the Yankee pitchers were Bill Stafford and Ralph Terry and you couldn't say the Yanks weren't trying.) Once the lead was gone, you'd have to bet Aunt Hattie's life insurance policy that might and the Yankees would prevail, but Howie Nunn got pinch hitter John (The Terrible) Blanchard to pop out and then Joe Christopher hit a ball over the head of Hector (What a Pair of Hands) Lopez in the ninth for a triple. Richie Ashburn knocked him in with a pinch single and the old folks cheered (6,277 of them, all paid) as though social security benefits had just been raised.

Now Stengel, who might have been at the peak of his career, was conducting an unusual press conference in the dugout after the game. In the spring reporters usually don't bother with postgame interviews. What's the sense of conducting a postmortem on an artificial corpse? But this time was history. How many times in the next ten years will the Mets beat the Yankees?

Casey Stengel winks during spring training in 1962. (Getty Images)

Mets manager Casey Stengel poses with Yankees stars Roger Maris (left) and Mickey Mantle during spring training on March 22, 1962. The Mets beat the Yankees 4–3 in an exhibition game that day. (AP Images)

The old manager took the straight lines and turned them into the greatest Stengel session since the day he was fired by the Yankees.

How come you shifted on Maris? (A perfect bit of strategy because Maris tried four times and didn't hit anything, not even a sports writer.)

Stengel gave himself the fingers in the eyes. "Twenty-twenty," he bragged. How many 71-year-old men could say the same?

How much do you like Christopher?

"Love him, love him," Stengel said, in the best falsetto. "Tonight I love him. Yesterday I didn't. Anyway I think he's got a bad back."

You think you'll get a wire of congratulations from Dan Topping?

"Oh sure. He's gonna take me back in eight years. He's got (George) Weiss worried."

"I'm glad we did good," he said. "It's good for the club. But we ain't so great. We didn't make the double play when it would have taken us out of it. My pitcher (Al Jackson) didn't throw the ball over to first base so they got down and broke up two double plays. It was a good game but we still did the same thing with men on base. I don't know when they're going to learn. I tell them to chop wood but they don't do it."

So it's back to the drawing board. But at least he knows the pilot model can beat the Yankees. It's a helluva start.

Casey Stengel signs autographs for fans before a spring training game in St. Petersburg, Florida, in 1962. (Getty Images)

September 24, 1969

	123	456	789	R H E
St. Louis Cardinals	000	000	000	0 4 1
New York Mets	500	010	00X	6 7 0

Playoff Expansion

METS CLINCH EASTERN DIVISION CHAMPIONSHIP BY VIC ZIEGEL

Last night, two hours and two minutes after the Mets had started the game with the Cardinals, Joe Torre rapped a ground ball to Bud Harrelson. The ball became a double play and gave the Mets a 6–0 victory that clinched first place.

The Mets in the dugout raced onto the field and surrounded Gary Gentry, the winning pitcher. The Mets who had been playing ran for the protection of the dugout. Several thousand fans, the crowd figure was 56,587, cleared the box and seat railings and chased after their heroes.

Infield sod was torn away for souvenirs. The rubber padding in the coaches' boxes and on deck circles was ripped out. Letters and numbers were pulled from the main and auxiliary scoreboards. A 16-year-old boy from Newark was sent to Elmhurst General Hospital for x-rays after he began climbing a ladder at the side of the scoreboard and fell an estimated 25 feet to the ground behind the outfield fence.

Meanwhile, in the clubhouse, in between the television cameras and tape recorders and microphones and lights and scores of reporters, the Mets were working hard to finish several cases of champagne. Some of it they drank.

Tug McGraw, running through the room, rubbed his fists into his eyes.

"They never told us this stuff burns," McGraw was hollering.

Tom Seaver, his hair slicked back with New York State grape, mounted the table Ralph Kiner and Lindsay Nelson were using to interview Johnny Murphy, the general manager, and M. Donald Grant, chairman of the Met board. Seaver emptied a bottle of champagne on all four.

Jerry Grote, wildest of all, jumped on another table and shouted, "Let's hear it for Leo."

"They said it couldn't be done," Ed Charles screamed. "Viva la Mets of New York. Viva, Viva. Doesn't anybody here speak Spanish?"

Nolan Ryan stood in the center of the room wearing a crown of shaving lather. A half-dozen Mets grabbed Rube Walker, the large pitching coach, and carried him toward the showers. The coach, riding very close to the clubhouse ceiling,

Manager Gil Hodges flashes a winning smile after the Mets clinched the National League East with a win over the St. Louis Cardinals. (Getty Images)

Mets players (from left) Ron Swoboda, Art Shamsky, and Ken Boswell lather up in shaving cream as they celebrate the Mets' National League East title. Jerry Grote (right) looks on. (Getty Images)

resembled nothing more than the whale at the Museum of Natural History. All the coaches, and several club officials and reporters, were hauled, kicking and screaming, into the showers. When Sal Marchiano of WCBS was swept into the shower, his camera crew followed.

Amos Otis upended a bottle of champagne inside the general manager's collar (Amos Otis?). Several of the Mets emptied cans of Yoo-Hoo over Yogi Berra. Joe McDonald, the director of minor league operations, grabbed Ken Boswell's arm and shouted, "Congratulations." Boswell said, "Thanks, Joe," hugged McDonald, and then threw a cupful of champagne into his face.

A half hour after the game, the players broke into loud, prolonged booking. The champagne was gone. Grote washed a television camera with beer. The catcher, Jerry Koosman, Boswell, and Duffy Dyer crept toward the manager's office carrying cans of beer. The room was packed with reporters and Gil Hodges was just about to begin a television interview.

He never saw the players.

They came up behind him, doused him with beer, turned him around, and pushed him out into the clubhouse. Ron Swoboda stood near his locker, wearing half a uniform and beatific expression, and shouted, "I'm so ha-a-a-py." Grote, leaping off a table, slammed two cups of yogurt over Walker's head.

The room seemed to be tilting when Boswell pulled away from a pack of yogurt freaks and said, "This is the greatest day of my life. This is better than winning at marbles when I was seven years old—and I never thought anything would be better than that."

This was the Mets' 96th victory of an incredible season. And they were winners last night before the first inning was over.

Donn Clendenon, the cleanup hitter, delivered a three-run home run. There was a walk to Swoboda, a home run by Charles, and Steve Carlton, who had struck out 19 Mets last week to set a major league record, was taken out of the game. A fifth-inning homer by Clendenon was the last Mets run. Gentry threw a strong four-hitter.

And when the game was over and the mad ball in the clubhouse was ending, Seaver stared across the room—at the empty champagne bottles, the beer cans, the towels, the flower petals scattered across the stained rug, the cans of soda, the turned-over glasses, the shaving cream cans—and said: "We had something different planned, something a little more dignified, something neater. But this'll do, this'll do."

> "They said it couldn't be done. Viva la Mets of New York. Viva, Viva. Doesn't anybody here speak Spanish?"
>
> —Ed Charles, Mets third baseman

	123	456	789	R H E
Atlanta Braves	200	020	000	4 8 1
New York Mets	001	231	00X	7 14 0

The Taste of Champagne

BOSWELL SAVORS PENNANT-WINNING FLAVOR BY VIC ZIEGEL

Ken Boswell spent the wettest part of an hour, after the Mets clinched first place in the Eastern Division, spilling champagne over the clubhouse rug, the man in the locker to his right, the neighbor to his left, reporters, front-office people, and anyone else who turned his way when Boswell called out, "Hey you."

That was not quite two weeks ago. Yesterday, when the Mets won the National League pennant, there was more champagne for the players. More to spill. More to *shoooosh* up with a finger kept over the mouth of the bottle. More laughs when streams of champagne shot against an innocent neck.

Someone, however, must have devoted the last two weeks to convincing Boswell that champagne is a sparkling, dry white table wine that is raised to the mouth, sipped, and swallowed.

The second baseman is learning. While most of the Mets partied with shaving cream and chocolate cake, Boswell stood in a quiet corner of the room and kept both hands around an almost-empty bottle of champagne. Occasionally, he would raise the bottle to his lips, sip as best he could, and swallow.

There was a look on his face that told you this was one bottle of champagne that was working perfectly.

A friend asked the second baseman about his afternoon, about the home run, the two singles, the flawless day in the field, and Boswell decided, at the very top of his lungs, "I can hit. Dagamm, I can hit. And next year…next year, I'm gonna win the Gold Glove.

"Man, I feel good, too good. I'm scared. They could send us to jail right now. I mean, how many years do they give for stealing a pennant?"

I can't believe this. I'll be honest with you. There was nobody on this club, I mean nobody, not even Gil thought this club would finish first when we were in Florida. What we wanted to do was finish the season strong and show people we had good material.

"Gil, man, he lets you know you're playing in the big leagues. He lets you know he never played on a loser and

Jerry Grote (left) and Rod Gaspar douse New York mayor John V. Lindsay with champagne after the Mets' 7–4 win over the Atlanta Braves to win the National League pennant. (AP Images)

Mets pitcher Nolan Ryan celebrates with catcher Jerry Grote after recording the final out of Game 3 of the National League Championship Series. Ryan pitched seven innings in relief of Gary Gentry to seal the victory. (AP Images)

doesn't want to manage a loser. I don't mean he walks around here saying that. He tells us through his teeth. He doesn't like us to make small mistakes, the stupid things that beat you.

"I hate to say anything about Atlanta, but they did things in the last three games that you shouldn't do in the big leagues."

There is another impressive swallow.

"Hey, I can't wait to play Baltimore. I'm glad they won today. Now we both get five days' rest. We both get fat and lazy and everybody can say, 'Wow, what a lousy World Series.'

"Yeah, yeah, they got great pitching. I know. But can't you see what's happening? Man, we're hitting balls behind us, on top of us, under us. What's the difference where they pitch us?

"Who do they have that's better than Hank Aaron? He may be the best man in baseball. Last year, when I was a rookie, the first time we played them, Hank hit a ball down the left-field line.

"When he got to second, I said, 'Ladies and gentlemen, that was double No. 8,765 for Hank Aaron.' He told me, 'No, kid, not that many yet.'

"But he said it like he meant to get them. Hell, he could hit from a wheelchair. I can't believe he ever goes 0-for-4.

"What did he get in this series? Ten RBIs, right? Isn't that right? When he got that double in the third inning, I walked over to him and said, 'Hey, Hank, let up on us. We're trying to win this thing.' I asked him what kind of food he was eating because I wanted to try the same stuff. He told me he couldn't eat anything for the last 24 hours.

"Hank's a gentleman, know that? I mean, what am I doing kidding around with him? I was born in Austin, Texas, and I went to the Astrodome when they played the first game there and I saw Mickey Mantle hit a home run.

"Hell, I was a kid then. It's hard to believe that there's some kids right now picking up a sport magazine and reading about Ken Boswell and knowing who I am. I used to read those magazines all the time, memorize them.

"Me and my friend, Larry Spillar, we'd get a cabin on a lake and swim and ski and read sports magazines and ask ourselves questions about the major leaguers. Our folks got real teed off. They said if we spent as much time with our school books as we did with those magazines, we'd have been valedictorians. Hey, they were right. We were down at the bottom of the class. Hey, there's nothing left in the bottle."

> "Man, I feel good, too good. I'm scared. They could send us to jail right now. I mean, how many years do they give for stealing a pennant?"
>
> —Ken Boswell, Mets second baseman

	1 2 3	4 5 6	7 8 9	R H E
Baltimore Orioles	0 0 3	0 0 0	0 0 0	3 5 2
New York Mets	0 0 0	0 0 2	1 2 X	5 7 0

It Isn't a Dream

MIRACLE METS WIN WORLD SERIES BY VIC ZIEGEL

The baseball that would make the Mets World Series champions began a brief flight toward Cleon Jones in left field. Met fans rushed past the ushers and ran to the box seat railings. Special police were leaping onto the field to prepare for the invasion.

And in the outfield, watching the ball drop, Jones remembers thinking, "Come down. Come on down, baby. I got you."

An instant later the baseball was in his glove and the game was over. The Mets were winners, 5–3. The World Series had ended in five games. The Mets were—and are—the No. 1 team in all baseball.

The Shea Stadium infield was hidden. There were hundreds of people on the grass, screaming, leaping, running along both sides of the baselines, surrounding the Met dugout, reaching out for the few players left in the open. A fan climbed the pitchers' mound and held a banner that read "What next?" And someone he didn't know grabbed him around the middle and they began a lopsided dance.

The outfield fences were covered with graffiti praising the Mets. The messages were in chalk, ink, crayon.

They should have used shoe polish.

The Mets beat the Orioles yesterday with five runs in the last three innings, the first time in the Series a team had won after falling behind.

Baltimore scored the first two runs of the game in the third inning on a single by Mark Belanger and a home run by Dave McNally, the Orioles' pitcher. Later in the same inning Frank Robinson slammed a long home run over the center-field wall.

The first five innings of the game were a bad time for the Mets. There was no hint of magic, no sign of divine guidance. The team of destiny seemed destined for nothing more than a trip to Baltimore.

And then the sixth inning began, the inning that will be remembered as long as baseball shoes are polished.

Frank Robinson was batting, with one out, when a pitch by Jerry Koosman seemed to hit Robinson and bounce away. A foul ball, the umpire decided. Robinson raged at the umpire,

Mets pitcher Jerry Koosman and catcher Jerry Grote celebrate after the final out of the Mets' Game 5 clinching win over the Orioles. (Getty Images)

and was joined by Earl Weaver, Baltimore's loud little manager.

"It hit me and then it hit the bat," Robinson protested.

The umpire, Lou DiMuro, did not agree. He motioned Robinson back to the plate. Robinson turned his back, walked into the dugout, and was out of sight for perhaps five minutes.

Robinson lowered his pants and the Baltimore trainer pressed ice against the red welt on the outfielder's thigh. It was only when DiMuro approached the dugout and said, "If you don't come out to hit, there'll have to be a pinch-hitter," that Robinson returned to the field. He struck out.

The first Met to bat in the sixth inning was Jones. And the first pitch from McNally landed against his right foot.

"I knew the ball hit me," Jones said. "No doubt about it. I started for first base but he said no."

The baseball kicked away from the batter, bounded into the Met dugout, and was caught by Jerry Grote.

"That's the turning point," Gil Hodges was to say later, "if the ball goes into their dugout instead of ours, we never see it again."

What Grote saw on the ball was a black smudge. He flipped it to Hodges and the manager brought it to DiMuro's attention. Shoe polish, Hodges pointed out. From a shoe, he explained. Jones' shoe, he insisted. The umpire agreed. Jones was sent to first base. And the 57,397 customers had another chance to watch Weaver argue.

"How do you know that's the same ball?" the manager asked the umpire.

"I watched it all the way," the umpire answered. (The argument was over. After the game, in the Mets clubhouse, Art Shamsky was to say, "We've worked on that play since spring training. Gil's had that ball with the shoe polish in his jacket all year.")

"They got that one right and Frank's wrong," was Weaver's last shot.

And so there was Jones, standing on first base, when Donn Clendenon, the very next hitter, slammed his third home run in the World Series. The Mets were a run behind.

An inning later, after a home run by Al Weis, the score was even, and the Mets were far ahead.

"The game was over," Ron Swoboda said. "Right then, I knew the game was over."

> "We've worked on that play since spring training. Gil's had that ball with the shoe polish in his jacket all year."
>
> —Art Shamsky, Mets outfielder

Mets second baseman Al Weis shakes hands with teammates after his seventh-inning home run in Game 5. Weis' homer tied the game 3–3. (Getty Images)

Eighth-inning doubles by Jones and Swoboda meant the winning run, and a pair of errors by Boog Powell and Eddie Watt—on a ground ball by Grote—scored Swoboda with the last run of the season.

A few more minutes and the team of destiny was celebrating in the clubhouse.

"Don't give me that destiny stuff," Swoboda was shouting, a can of beer in his hand. "Destiny brings you just so far, but destiny doesn't win you a hundred games. Destiny doesn't win you a playoff. And destiny doesn't win four games for you in a best-of-seven series."

Then how can anyone explain the Mets—the 100:1 nowhere men when the season began, the underdogs for every one of the World Series games—wading in champagne in the world champion clubhouse?"

"Haven't you heard?" Cleon Jones said. "Good pitching stops good hitting every time."

371

Cleon Jones catches Davey Johnson's fly ball for the
last out of the 1969 World Series. (Getty Images)

The world championship banner flies over Shea Stadium as fans storm the field after the Mets' series-clinching Game 5 victory. (Getty Images)

Mets fan Karl Ehrhardt, better known as the Sign Man, holds up an appropriate sign during the Mets' Game 5 win. (AP Images)

Mets pitcher Jerry Koosman jumps into the arms of catcher Jerry Grote after the Mets' clinching win. Third baseman Ed Charles joins the celebration on the mound. (AP Images)

	1 2 3	4 5 6	7 8 9	R H E
San Diego Padres	0 1 0	0 0 0	0 0 0	1 2 0
New York Mets	1 0 1	0 0 0	0 0 X	2 4 0

How Seaver Did the Trick

ACE STRIKES OUT 19 IN WIN BY PAUL ZIMMERMAN

The memory of July 9, 1969, hung over Tom Seaver yesterday, just before his 19 strikeouts moved him into the record books alongside Steve Carlton.

He had lost a perfect game that night in '69 when Jimmy Qualls singled with one out in the ninth. He beat the Cubs, 4–0.

Yesterday the count on the Padres' Al Ferrara was 1–2, with two out in the ninth, the Mets leading 2–1, and 18 Seaver strikeouts in the book.

"The right pitch to Ferrara would have been an outside slider," Seaver said. "But I decided to challenge him with my best pitch—a fastball.

"I went for the strikeout. I figured, well, I may never come this close again. I better go after it. When he first came up I was just thinking about winning the game. I mean, he's a fastball hitter and he hit a fastball for a homer in the second inning (a 2–1 pitch that bounced off the top of the left-field bullpen wall).

"But the last one I gave him in the ninth was low—just where I wanted it—and he missed it. It was a good pitch. Actually, the last two pitches to him were fastballs."

"Him against me—his best shot against my best shot," said Ferrara, who had plagued the Mets with seven homers against them one season.

"He was going for the strikeout. I was going for the downs. He won."

Seaver had just struck out Clarence Gaston for No. 18, one short of Carlton's major league record. It was Seaver's ninth K in a row, which gave him that record. Ferrara became No. 10.

"The first two pitches I gave Ferrara were sliders," Seaver said. "The next two were fastballs."

Slider number one was a strike on the outside corner and Ferrara took a half swing at it. The second one missed low and away, and plate ump Harry Wendelstedt, caught up in the drama of the occasion, shook his head no.

"That's when I went for the strikeout—when I had him 1–1," Seaver said.

It was a low-key type of classic—weekday afternoon, early

Tom Seaver gets a kiss from his wife, Nancy, after striking out 19 San Diego Padres on April 22, 1970. (Getty Images)

Mets catcher Jerry Grote catches the Tom Seaver pitch as San Diego's Al Ferrara strikes out to end the game on April 22, 1970. Seaver tied the major league record with 19 strikeouts. He fanned the last 10 batters he faced. (Getty Images)

season game, expansion team, etc. Seaver took the whole thing calmly, sipping a beer, and then another, dissecting his performance almost clinically. In his locker, twenty feet away, was the 1969 Cy Young Award, which had been given to him before the game.

"When they flashed the news on the scoreboard that I had tied Nolan Ryan's club strikeout record at 15 (eighth inning), I thought I had 10 or 11," Seaver said. "I couldn't believe I had as many as 15.

"The emotion I felt today wasn't as great as last year against the Cubs, when I had a perfect game with one out in the ninth. Several reasons—this one was against an expansion club, and the Cubs were in first place then. And that one was a night game with 59,000 people in the stands." (Yesterday's attendance was 21,694 total, 14,197 paid.)

"I'm not really blasé. But this doesn't exhilarate me as much as a perfect game would have. That's the one I wish I had."

Seaver retired the last 16 Padres in order, 12 of them on K's. During his 10-strikeout streak at the end, he hit a perfect groove—fastball and outside slider.

"That one groove he hit," said San Diego's minor league pitching instructor, Johnny Podres, "he'll never throw that hard again in his life."

"That's what Ron Santo said last year after that game against the Cubs," Seaver said. "He said I'd never throw that hard again. Maybe Podres and Santo ought to get together and have dinner."

> "When they flashed the news on the scoreboard that I had tied Nolan Ryan's club strikeout record at 15 (eighth inning), I thought I had 10 or 11, I couldn't believe I had as many as 15."
>
> —Tom Seaver

	123	456	789	RHE
San Francisco Giants	000	040	000	490
New York Mets	400	010	00X	540

Willie Writes an Extra Chapter

MAYS HOMERS IN RETURN TO NEW YORK BY MILTON GROSS

A publishing house, which was not interested before, is now interested in a new autobiography of Willie Mays. "Now you got something more to sell," said Willie to the author. "You got two things. No, you got three—a beginning, a middle, and an end."

It should be fiction and forget the end. Just think about the new beginning. Willie did, as he circled the bases yesterday for the 617th home run of his career after his 10,431st official at-bat, his first homer of the season in his first game as a Met to beat his old Giants 5–4. "I thought," said Mays, "what a way to start. I remembered the first hit I got for the Giants was a homer and we won the pennant and I break in with the Mets with a home run. Gee, it would be nice to win a pennant here."

As Willie rounded second after his fifth-inning leadoff 3-and-2 homer off Don Carrithers, a right-hander no less, his former teammate, Tito Fuentes, called to him, "Bat Boy."

That's an old gag between them. When Willie used to hit them for the Giants and knew they were going out, he'd flip the bat to the boy and the Giants' bench would yell "Bat Boy."

As he rounded third, Willie looked into the visiting dugout. "All I could see was 'Giants' on the shirts and I played for that team 21 years. I don't know what they're thinking, but they traded me and maybe they were thinking I couldn't play any more."

What they were thinking was best expressed by coach Joey Amalfitano, Willie's teammate for many seasons.

"You couldn't write a script better than that, could you?" said Joey. "Dammit, I'd pay to see that guy play. He hit the hell out of it. What a time to do it."

"On a scale of one to 10 for drama, I'd have to rate that homer about 12," said Bud Harrelson.

"Just watching him do it," said Jim Fregosi, "gave me a thrill. He starts his career in New York. He's traded back. He's playing against his old team and he hits the homer to win the game. What bigger thing could it be? It's an almost unbelievable situation."

Willie Mays appears in a Mets uniform for the first time on May 13, 1972. (AP Images)

Willie Mays watches his fifth-inning home run sail over the left-field fence at Shea Stadium. Mays' homer in his third Mets at-bat provided the margin of victory as the Mets topped Mays' former team, the San Francisco Giants, 5–4. (Getty Images)

"I got news for you," said Harrelson, who struck out after Willie's homer. "It was a tough act to follow. I think that kid is going to be all right."

Maybe some of the Mets were wondering before. There are some who seem to resent the attention and money he's getting, but not after that debut.

As a matter of fact some of them didn't quite know how to greet him after Rusty Staub's grand-slam homer in the first had been wiped out by a Giants' four-run inning in the fifth. They stood at the edge of the dugout seemingly stunned, then began to shake his hand and pound his back. It was the first pitch he hit fairly in the game after walking as leadoff and striking out in the second. In the seventh, Willie walked again and then was out stealing on what he mistook for a hit-and-run sign.

"He thought there was one on," said manager Yogi Berra, "but there wasn't. He's new and doesn't know the signs yet. He came back to the dugout mad at himself and asked me if the hit and run was on. I said no."

Willie had seven plays at first base but the virtuosity of the man who started because lefty Sam McDowell opened for the Giants showed in the eighth with Garry Maddox on second and two outs. Pinch-hitter Dave Rader grounded to Harrelson. Bud threw inside the base. Willie gloved it one-handed and swept a tag at the runner. "That's just the way Willie McCovey got his arm broken," said Berra. "If I made that play I'd get my arm broken."

"You don't think of things like that at a time like that," said Mays. "That man gets on, it's a bad spot. It was just a play that had to be made that way."

"I thought he made a helluva play," said Harrelson. "It was a bad throw but he didn't think anything of it. He thought it was routine."

"Any expression on his face when he scored after the homer?" Bud was asked.

"He's been around there before," said Harrelson. "He hit that goddamn thing so low I thought it would take the top of the fence off. Plus their outfielder Garry Maddox out there is nine feet tall."

Which is the height Willie should have felt but he was so nervous before the game, he didn't want to talk about it in advance. He pretended not to be tense, invited Tommie Agee and Cleon Jones to come with him to his tailor at Petrocelli's and discussed the price of his gray boots. Anything not baseball.

"I was so nervous," said Willie, "I didn't think I'd hit the baseball." He was so nervous, in fact, that his first throw before the game went over Fregosi's head. And when he came onto the field, he pointed to first base and asked Umpire Mel Steiner: "Is that first base?" Steiner said: "That's first base."

Willie knew where home plate was, though, and when he homered he knew immediately he had hit it too hard for Maddox to get to the sinking line drive. One more thing. It was his 1,860th RBI, which ties the late Mel Ott of the Giants for third place on the NL All-Time list. The next one and even Ottey will be wiped out but this 41-year-old with the flare for dramatics will continue to bring former Giant fan and owner Mrs. Joan Payson to her feet in her private box.

She bought a collector's item but the old boy isn't ready to be stored in a case—yet.

	123	456	789	R	H	E
Cincinnati Reds	001	010	000	2	7	1
New York Mets	200	041	00X	7	13	1

Fans Sour the Champagne

RIOTS BREAK OUT AS METS TAKE PENNANT BY MAURY ALLEN

Another Mets pennant, another cast of thousands tearing up Shea Stadium, another small riot threatening pregnant women and small children, another beautiful October day in New York, New York, that wonderful town.

The Mets beat the Reds 7–2 for the National League pennant yesterday afternoon and the joy of the afternoon was tempered by the anger of the visitors.

"I'm not angry," said Sparky Anderson. "I'm just ashamed. I'm ashamed that I live in this country. I'm not too sure New York is in this country."

The Mets were two outs away from ending the game when some of the natives grew too restless to wait. They stormed the dugouts, taunted the Reds, pushed women and children, cursed and kicked police.

Executive vice president of the Reds, Bob Howsam, left his box and asked the nearest cop for more protection from the fans.

"What can I do?" the cop said.

A barrier in front of the Cincinnati box was pushed over and Mrs. George Ballou, wife of the Cincinnati doctor, was injured. She was evacuated to safety through the freedom passage in the Reds dugout. She was followed by the rest of the Cincinnati official party, including Senator Robert Taft.

Even Tom Seaver, who answered all the questions with his sparkling performance, was upset by the disgraceful show.

"It's a shame," said Seaver. "It's a disgrace. We work hard all year to win the pennant and then we have to stand around because they want to rush on the field." At 4:50 PM on a gorgeous October day in Flushing, New York, Dan Driessen grounded to John Milner at first base. The fans and Tug McGraw, who had relieved Seaver for the final two outs, raced for the bag. McGraw won by a step and didn't stop running until he was atop a wooden platform in the clubhouse yelling, "You gotta believe, you gotta believe, you gotta believe."

Mets manager Yogi Berra exchanges pleasantries with his Reds counterpart, Sparky Anderson, before a 1973 National League Championship Series game at Cincinnati's Riverfront Stadium. The Mets beat the defending National League champion Reds in five games. (Getty Images)

Shea Stadium personnel carry off a spectator who was injured when he and others poured onto the field from the stands following the Mets' pennant-clinching win over the Cincinnati Reds. (AP Images)

Now the Mets can rest a day while Baltimore and Oakland settle the American League thing. If the Orioles win, the Amtrak World Series begins Saturday in Baltimore at 1 PM. If the A's win, the trans-continental World Series begins in California Saturday at 4 PM New York time.

It will be Jon Matlack in the opener for the Mets.

"I'll think about that tomorrow," said Yogi Berra.

Berra sat in his office and calmly accepted congratulations for his team's triumph. He showed some temper only when asked about Seaver's performance on three days' rest.

"You guys," he said, "made a big deal of Seaver's short rest. He can pitch anytime. I'd like to have four Seavers."

General Manager Bob Scheffing, a man who exuded patience all summer and stayed in the kitchen for the heat, simply smiled at the triumph and went about his business. He was watching the Oakland-Baltimore game carefully on television.

In the Mets clubhouse the celebrations and demonstrations were subdued compared to the riotous carryings-on in Chicago when the division was clinched.

Perhaps the joy was best expressed by Ed Kranepool, who started in place of the injured Rusty Staub, and delivered the two-run, first-inning single that gave Seaver his opening lead. The Reds tied it at 2–2 in the fifth but the Mets won it with four crazy runs in the bottom of the fifth.

"I got the Mets started today," he said, "just like I did 12 years ago with my bonus."

Kranepool was entitled to the satisfaction of the moment after all the down years as a Met and the up year of 1969.

"I was in last-place for seven years. I know what it was like. When we were down this summer I told (Donald) Grant we weren't a last place team. We had self-pride. That's what got us going. This is satisfying because everybody was down on me, the fans, the management, Yogi. But I knew I could hit. Put me out there every day, pitcher, catcher, anyplace, I'll always hit."

Kranepool said he took great joy again from watching teammates pour champagne down Willie Mays'

> "It's a shame, it's a disgrace. We work hard all year to win the pennant and then we have to stand around because they want to rush on the field."
>
> —Tom Seaver

throat. Mays had batted for Kranepool in the weird fifth and got a fluke infield single.

"This was for Willie," Kranepool said. "He came in as a champion in 1951 and we wanted him to go out as a champion. I told him we'd get him drunk three times. We got him drunk in Chicago and we got him drunk today and we'll get him drunk again after we beat Reggie Jackson or the Birds or whoever. What time does the bus for Oakland leave?"

Kranepool admitted that things looked bleak in July and August. The Mets were down 12½ games in early August and last as late as Aug. 30.

"We coulda folded," he said. "We coulda packed our bags and gone home. We didn't because we were professionals. We have pride. We wanted the money and the prestige."

Kranepool's bases-loaded single gave Seaver two quick runs in the first.

It wasn't quite enough for the Big Mets Machine but Seaver wasn't about to be beaten on this day.

"Honestly," Seaver said, "I got ready for this game as a routine game. I was so drained emotionally from not winning on Tuesday I had nothing left."

After the Mets went ahead 7–2 in the fifth Seaver suddenly felt the impact of the game, the final pennant-winning game.

"It hit me like a brick wall," he said. "I finally understood what it meant."

He was throwing curves and off-speed pitches earlier. Then he started to throw the hard stuff. The Reds were finished. If it were not for fan interference, Seaver certainly would have completed the game.

It didn't matter. He had won the biggest game of his career and the Mets will be in Oakland or Baltimore Saturday because of him.

At the end it was Tug McGraw, drenched in sweat and champagne, his fireman's hat on his head, his eyes wide open, his heart singing, who rallied the troops. "You gotta believe, you gotta believe."

Now I believe.

October 1, 1985

	1 2 3	4 5 6	7 8 9	10 11	R H E
New York Mets	0 0 0	0 0 0	0 0 0	0 1	1 8 1
St. Louis Cardinals	0 0 0	0 0 0	0 0 0	0 0	0 4 1

Ya Gotta Believe!

DARRYL, METS DEAL CARDS STUNNING BLOW BY BOB KLAPISCH

The home run stunned Busch Stadium into absolute silence. In the instant Darryl Strawberry cut St. Louis' lead to two games, you could almost hear Whitey Herzog ask himself, "Is this really happening?"

In one powerful cut off a Ken Dayley curveball, Strawberry beat the Cardinals 1–0 in 11 innings last night. It ended the game that St. Louis, "Wanted real bad. Their must-win," Davey Johnson said.

Why? Because John Tudor, the Cards' magician, pitched. Now a two-game deficit…and Dwight Gooden goes tonight. The Mets are more than alive. They're whispering about a miracle.

"The pressure is on them now," said Ron Darling, who threw nine zeroes—the best game of his two-year career. "Everyone says we're out of it, we have no chance. Well, we beat them with Tudor and now they have to see Dwight."

"The pendulum," Johnson said, "has begun to swing the other way."

Maybe. As Keith Hernandez said, "Ask me after Dwight pitches. If we beat them tonight…well, I don't want to even talk about it. This was big, man. Real big."

It was a night that Tudor and Darling matched zeroes for nine. A night when the Mets blew a suicide squeeze in the seventh…and blew a no-one-out-Gary-Carter-on-second rally in the ninth…and allowed Tommy Herr to reach second on Mookie Wilson's two-base error in the 11th.

But this was also a night the Cards couldn't score on Darling with runners on first and second in the seventh and one out…and couldn't score off Jesse Orosco with men on first and second and Jack Clark up in the 10th.

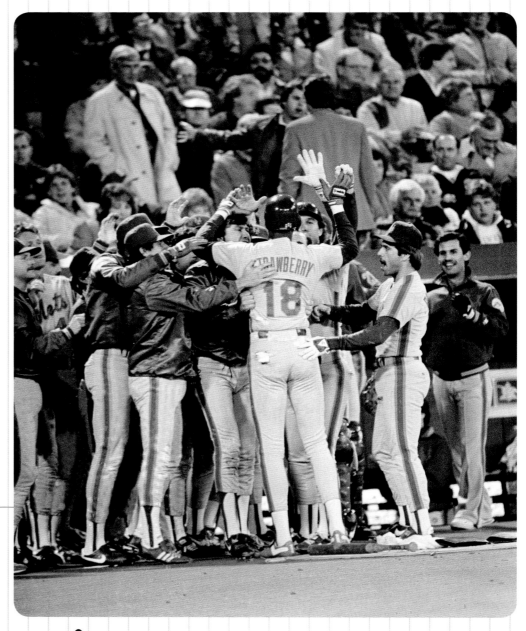

Darryl Strawberry is congratulated by teammates at home plate after his solo home run in the 11th inning gave the Mets a 1–0 win over the St. Louis Cardinals on October 1, 1985. The win pulled the Mets within one game of the Cardinals in the National League East standings. The Cardinals ultimately won the National League pennant before losing the World Series to the Kansas City Royals in seven games. (AP Images)

Ron Darling throws a pitch against the Cardinals at Busch Stadium on October 1, 1985. Darling threw nine scoreless innings. (AP Images)

"What else do you call this except baseball? Real baseball," an exhausted Carter said. "I'm not saying we're going to win this thing. But games like this… that's how teams win pennants."

With power.

"I can't remember hitting a home run this important since high school," Strawberry said. "I saw the pitch up in my zone, and I swear my eyes lit up. It was right there."

The 11th inning began with Dayley fanning both Hernandez and Carter. This, after Tudor had ruled the Mets like house pets for 10 innings. "Were we down? Sure, a little," Strawberry said.

"Tudor overmatched us last time [a 1–0, 10-inning win at Shea Sept. 11] and he overmatched us again tonight. His change, his fastball…he didn't make any mistakes."

But Dayley (4–4) did. A fastball up and in, ball one. A breaking ball, down and away, strike one.

"I had a feeling he was coming back with another breaking pitch," Strawberry said. "With a power hitter, you can't make the mistake of getting the ball up."

Strawberry was right. Another high deuce, a sign hung around its neck that read: "Crush me." Dayley disgustedly said, "It was right there, down the middle."

Strawberry took it nearly 500 feet over the wall in right, and—save for some 11th-inning drama from the Cards—the Mets were safe.

Safe and beyond the reach of second-guessers. Logic said Johnson had to throw Gooden last night. First game, big series, best pitcher. Right?

"But how could I have done that to Ronnie?" Johnson said. "It would've been like me telling him, 'I don't trust you.' I have confidence in Ron Darling. Shoot, we would've never gotten here without him."

"Hearing people talk about that offended me a little," Darling said. "But I knew I had to throw a big game. We were facing Tudor. I knew I had to shut them down. That guy is awesome."

After Carter led off the ninth with a bloop double over first, Tudor humiliated Strawberry. First on a 2–2 fastball up and in that Darrell Porter and Terry Pendleton let drop in foul territory. Given another life, Strawberry watched helplessly at an off-speed change for strike three.

"His change? I saw 75 percent change-ups," Wally Backman said. "You come back to the bench asking yourself, 'Can Tudor really be this good?' After a while, you just hope Ronnie can hold them down long enough to get Tudor out of the game."

Darling did, which brought the Mets to the 10th and 11th. First, Orosco (8–6) got out of a first and second jam by inducing pinch-hitter Clark to fly to right.

> "I can't remember hitting a home run this important since high school."
>
> —Darryl Strawberry

Then, with Herr on third after Mookie's error and a ground out, Orosco got Ivan DeJesus to fly out to center to end the game. With Tudor out of the way, the Mets are counting on Gooden as a lock over Joaquin Andujar. Rick Aguilera goes tomorrow against Danny Cox.

Pressure? Depends on whom you ask.

"Who the bleep is in first place?" Herzog asked testily.

"Yeah," Strawberry countered, "but who has to face Doc?"

September 17, 1986

	1 2 3	4 5 6	7 8 9	R	H	E
Chicago Cubs	0 0 0	0 0 0	0 2 0	2	6	3
New York Mets	0 0 2	0 1 0	1 0 X	4	11	0

How Sweet It Is!

METS ICE NL EAST BY BOB KLAPISCH

The clubhouse was a champagne jungle. Korbel in your eyes. Andre in your face. Great Western in your pants. After 13 years, the Mets threw a party that'll leave Queens with a Rest-of-September Hangover.

Actually, an upper-deck banner said it all: Finally. The Mets were officially coronated the Eastern Division champions with a 4–2 win over the Cubs last night. Finally.

Outside, 20,000 fans were on the field—overrunning the outmanned security force. Inside, Darryl Strawberry was drowning Mayor Koch in Andre. Ron Darling's entire torso was covered in shaving cream. Davey Johnson was hoisted into the shower by a four-man escort. Roger McDowell was using his pants pocket as a Korbel holster.

Finally.

"This is for the fans. They wanted it. They deserve it," Keith Hernandez said, shouting over the bedlam. "We wanted this so badly…to do it at home is so fitting. I can't tell you how it feels."

"This is the greatest day of my life," said Dwight Gooden, the complete-game winner in the Mets' first division clincher since 1973. "I was standing on the mound with two out, two strikes. I had to take a deep breath and tell myself, 'Just relax.' That's how excited I was."

This moment's been coming since June—or July if you accepted Whitey Herzog's surrender. Spontaneous? Hardly. But it was wild, almost frightening. When Wally Backman flipped Chico Walker's grounder to Hernandez for the final out at 10:15 PM, Shea went berserk.

Backman headed for the mound. "But within four steps I was knocked down by four or five guys. They took my hat, and they were trying to get my glove. Another couple of fans said, 'Follow us. We'll take you to the dugout.' I couldn't believe it: they really did."

Gooden was mobbed at the mound—not only by teammates, but by fans. Within moments after retiring Walker, the Doctor was down and unable to escape. "I was scared. For five

A group of Mets players celebrate on the Shea Stadium mound after beating the Cubs to clinch the National League East title. The players are (from left) Randy Myers, Bob Ojeda, Ron Darling, Rick Aguilera, Ed Hearn, Darryl Strawberry, and Howard Johnson. (AP Images)

Mets fans pull up pieces of the turf as they celebrate after the Mets clinched the National League East title on September 17, 1986. (AP Images)

minutes, I felt people pounding on me, and I couldn't get up," Gooden said. "After a while, someone let me up. I don't know who it was, but I headed right for the clubhouse."

Actually, the saviors were Hernandez and Kevin Mitchell, who along with three cops rushed to the mound. "We got there and started screaming at the fans, 'Look who's down there!'" Hernandez said. "There was definitely Mel [Stottlemyre] and Aggie [Rick Aguilera]. I don't know who else. The fans realized who it was. They parted like the Red Sea for Moses."

Still, the Mets harbored no ill feelings toward the Shea denizens—even though an hour-long celebration left the infield with several bald spots. Grounds crew chief Pete Flynn glumly said, "This is worse than 1969." He and 20 workers labored through the night to repair the damage in time for the Mets to play the Cubs this afternoon.

From the start, the atmosphere was electric. Gooden (15–6) was staked to an early 3–0 lead against Dennis Eckersley. Two of the RBIs came from rookie Dave Magadan—replacing Hernandez, who was ill with a virus. Magadan, Lou Piniella's cousin, said he felt like "an outsider" before last night. Such is life for an insecure rookie.

Talk about timing: Magadan had run-scoring singles in the third and fifth innings—enough room for Gooden to allow a two-run homer to Rafael Palmeiro in the eighth.

That narrowed the Mets' lead to 4–2. No matter, said Davey Johnson,

who decided, "We lost [four straight] on the road because fate wanted us to win it here. I knew we were going to win it tonight. It was better this way."

Finally. The Mets will eventually devote their attention to the Astros, but first will take a two- or three-day sabbatical. Johnson says, "I'm going to give my regulars some time off, while I look at younger guys."

Smart manager. The Met regulars won't get near a Louisville Slugger today. That's how intensely they partied. The clubhouse carpet was soaked with champagne. Beer. Shaving cream. Name it and the Mets wore it.

"This is great. So great," said Howard Johnson. "I went through the same thing with the Tigers two years ago, but this feels better. It's a better organization here. Better manager. I love this. What else can you say?"

Only…finally.

> "I was standing on the mound with two out, two strikes. I had to take a deep breath and tell myself, 'Just relax.' That's how excited I was."
>
> —Dwight Gooden

	1 2 3	4 5 6	7 8 9	10 11 12	13 14 15 16	R	H	E
New York Mets	0 0 0	0 0 0	0 0 3	0 0 0	0 1 0 3	7	11	0
Houston Astros	3 0 0	0 0 0	0 0 0	0 0 0	0 1 0 2	6	11	1

Clincher Is One for the Books

AMAZIN' 16-INNING WIN VAULTS METS INTO SERIES BY BOB KLAPISCH

Call it simply The Game. It will never need another description. The Game. That's all you have to say.

It took 4:42—the longest contest in playoff history. It took 16 innings. It left 24 men exhausted beyond words, too tired to drink more than a sip of champagne.

The Game. The Mets' 7–6 win over the Astros that ended the NLCS in six and earned the Mets the right to meet Boston in their first World Series in 13 years.

Exhaustion. Fatigue. Relief. What else could the Mets feel after Bob Ojeda's first-inning nightmare? After being three outs away from facing Mike Scott in Game 7? Within one pitch blowing a three-run lead in the 16th?

How much could any human—player or spectator—endure?

"Watching this game was unbelievable. Maybe I had a heart attack, I don't know. I'm not sure," said Wally Backman. He was holding a champagne bottle, but not even bothering to lift it to his lips.

"I think I aged 10 years in the last two days. I'm so numb.... I don't even know what I'm thinking anymore. Say it this way: this was the greatest game I ever played and ever saw."

"I know the whole National League wanted us to lose," said a pale Keith Hernandez. "Right now, I don't give a bleep what they think. They have to respect us now. This was the greatest playoff game ever played, and it ranks with the '75 World Series. I mean that. Without this, 108 wins wouldn't have meant anything."

The Astros were numb in defeat. A little bitter, too. Can they be blamed? Astro starter Bob Knepper said softly, "I felt we should have beaten them. I feel we should be in the Series. Not them."

Knepper fell three outs short. Without Knepper's failure, Roger McDowell wouldn't have thrown five shutout innings. And Ray Knight wouldn't have driven home the winning run in the 16th. And Jesse Orosco wouldn't have—barely—withstood the most frightening moment in the Mets' 25-year history.

Jesse Orosco leaps off the mound in celebration after striking out Kevin Bass in the bottom of the 16th inning of Game 6 of the 1986 National League Championship Series. (AP Images)

Len Dykstra leaps onto a pile of teammates to celebrate the Mets' 1986 National League pennant. Dykstra's pinch-hit triple leading off the ninth inning ignited the Mets' comeback win. (AP Images)

"No one wanted to see Scott again," said Lenny Dykstra. "He manhandled us. He was incredible and we knew he would be again."

"Dominated" is the word Darryl Strawberry chose. "Every one in this locker room is glad it ended today, Scott was that tough. Now he can't scuff the ball again until next year."

Three outs. That's all the Astros needed to get to Game 7. Three outs, and Knepper was mowing through the Mets "like we were babies," said Dykstra.

Ron Darling flatly said, "I didn't think we had a chance to win this. Not a chance at all."

Three outs and down 3–0. Johnson chose to pinch-hit Dykstra—an unorthodox lefty-lefty gamble.

"I wanted to put the bat on the ball," said Dykstra. "Put it in play, at least not strike out. I didn't want him to throw the ball by me."

And here it began: Dykstra lifted a massive 0–2 count triple over Billy Hatcher's head in center. Mookie Wilson followed with a single, which glanced over the top of Bill Doran's glove, cutting the Astros' lead to 3–1. Kevin Mitchell's ground ball put Wilson on second.

Knepper foolishly tried to challenge Hernandez with a fastball—which Hernandez ripped up the gap in right-center. The Mets were closing, down 3–2. Hal Lanier sensed this. He lifted Knepper and summoned Dave Smith to face Gary Carter. Smith walked Carter and Strawberry, loading the bases.

He went 1–2 on Ray Knight…and threw a fastball an eyelash outside. Catcher Alan Ashby slammed his glove on the ground, shouting at home-plate umpire Fred Brocklander, "That was a strike!"

Knight wheeled around. He was in Ashby's face instantly. "That was not a strike," Knight shouted. "You don't even know what a strike is." Dickie Thon approached menacingly, taunting Knight. Knight asked, "Are you talking to me?" Thon said, "Yeah, you. Bleep you." Knight replied, "Bleep you, too, pal. You better get back to shortstop."

The moment was huge, enormous. Smith's next pitch, a 2–2 fastball, was low and away and Knight drilled it to center—a sacrifice fly that sent the game into extra innings.

For the next five innings, McDowell threw zeroes. He was operating on fear. "Twice this year, we'd come back in the ninth inning, and both times I lost the game," said McDowell. "I didn't want it to happen again."

Zeroes. And more zeroes. Would it end? Could it? Yes—or so it seemed when Backman lashed a 14th-inning single off Lopez.

The Astros responded with a one-out homer from Hatcher off Jesse Orosco.

Orosco watched the ball sail into the left-field foul pole, fighting his anger. "I told myself, 'It's not over. Not yet.'" Hernandez went to the mound and said simply, "Hold 'em, Jesse. Don't give in. We will score."

Sixteenth inning. Strawberry lifted a massive pop-up behind second off Lopez. "I knew it would be tough to catch because I saw Hatcher move back," Strawberry said. "I wanted to be on second."

> "Watching this game was unbelievable. Maybe I had a heart attack, I don't know. I'm not sure."
>
> —Wally Backman, Mets second baseman

Knight again punched a single to right, an RBI single that sparked the Mets' three-run rally. Backman drew a walk from Jeff Calhoun, who followed with two wild pitches and allowed Dykstra an RBI single.

Three runs, and the Mets were safe.

Were they? With one out in the 16th…Davey Lopes walked, Bill Doran singled, Hatcher singled—one run. Denny Walling hit into a 3–6 force, but Glenn Davis lifted a soft, looping single to center. Another run. Mets 7, Astros 6.

A panicked conference followed on the mound:

Backman to Orosco: "You're the best, Jesse. You are the best. Go with your slider. Throw it."

Backman, later: "I was scared. We all were. But I'll say this for Jesse. A lot of guys would've folded up and said, 'I don't want to be here.' Not him."

Knight to Orosco: "This game is in your hands. Give me your best. Don't give up. Do it, Jesse."

Knight, later: "It was pretty heated out there. Jesse was getting apprehensive. Yeah, I was nervous. I was scared."

Hernandez to Gary Carter: "If you call for one fastball to [Kevin] Bass I'll come to home plate and fight you."

Was Orosco nervous? Could any human not be? "Sure I was," he said. "But I told myself, 'You have the ball. You have the power. Don't let these guys down.'"

Slider. Slider. Slider. Slider. Slider. Slider. Six times, and Bass was out on strikes. He called it "an empty feeling." Nothing more.

Bass watched helplessly as the Mets converged on the mound. They were delirious, pounding backs, high-fiving…they'd done it.

"Are there words for this?" Carter asked breathlessly. "I don't think so. This game was so…I don't know. It was so…I don't know. Unbelievable."

Unbelievable. The Game will always be remembered that way.

October 27, 1986

	1 2 3	4 5 6	7 8 9	R H E
Boston Red Sox	0 3 0	0 0 0	0 2 0	5 9 0
New York Mets	0 0 0	0 0 3	3 2 X	8 10 0

We're No. 1

AMAZIN'S RALLY PAST RED SOX TO WIN SERIES BY BOB KLAPISCH

They spoke thousands of words—but in reality they were speechless. The Mets were too numb to make sense. They chugged champagne. They hugged each other. They wept. They exchanged looks that said: the world is ours.

It took seven exhausting games, but the World Series ended last night at 11:26. It was the Mets who out the Red Sox, 8–5. It was the Mets who scored eight runs in the final three innings—capturing their first world championship since 1969. It is the Mets who can now shake their fists at the National League.

Finally? Yes. Finally.

"Regardless of the jealousy, the envy, the hatred that exists for us, we have to be considered a great team now. We have to," Gary Carter said. "We showed our true character in this Series. This team is…I don't know. I really don't know what to say."

Carter—like every other champagne-drenched body in the Met clubhouse—will be emotionally spent for weeks. The post-game riot in the locker room was more relief than celebration.

It was Wally Backman high-fiving Howard Johnson, saying only: "We did it, didn't we." It was Keith Hernandez to Jesse Orosco: "You're a man, Jess." It was Darryl Strawberry to Ray Knight: "I love you."

How many times had we seen it? What did we learn from Game 6 in Houston? Character. And Game 6 at Shea? Character. The Mets used the word in every breath. And who can argue?

Bruce Hurst owned them for five innings with a 3–0 lead but Strawberry said, "We were sitting in the dugout telling ourselves, 'We can get this guy. He's not sharp.' No one on this team thought he was going to beat us again."

And then came the sixth-, seventh-, and eighth-inning explosions that left the Red Sox crushed. John McNamara went through six pitchers, looking for a way to contain the Mets. There were no answers. Not last night. Not in 1986.

Destiny? "Yeah, we were destined to win this," said Ron

Jesse Orosco drops to his knees in celebration after closing out the Red Sox to win Game 7 of the 1986 World Series. (New York Post)

Mets players celebrate on the Shea Stadium field after winning the 1986 World Series. (New York Post)

Darling—who lasted only 3⅔ innings and admitted, "I had nothing."

"We didn't even play well and we won. We may not have even deserved to win—and we did. Yeah. I'd call it destiny."

Destiny: Sid Fernandez bailed out Darling, threw zeroes until the sixth, and fanned four Red Sox hitters. Boston's offense vanished.

Destiny: Hurst simply lost his stuff in the sixth. With one out, Lee Mazzilli singled, Mookie Wilson singled, Tim Teufel walked, and Hernandez came to the plate.

Hernandez was hitting .251 in the postseason. He'd heard grumblings about only four RBIs in 13 games. But the bases were loaded now. His chance was in front of him.

"I told my brother in the morning, 'Gary, if there is any justice in the world, I'll get up in a tight situation and get a big hit.'" Hernandez said. "I've hit so many balls right at people.... I looked at it this way: I knew Hurst was going on three days' rest, and he wasn't as sharp as Game 5. He was pitching the way he did in Game 1 [also on three days' rest]. Mostly fastballs. I figured on the same pattern."

Hernandez smiled. "That was a big, big hit."

This big: a fastball. A two-run single, roped up the gap in left-center. It brought the Mets within 3–2 and told them: Hurst is mortal tonight.

Why? How? Wasn't this the same Hurst who'd ruled the Mets like house pets for 17 innings? Yes, it was. But this time, Hurst was working on just three days' rest—McNamara's gamble in passing over Oil Can Boyd.

To a man, the Mets said Hurst's fastball was a little fatter than Games 1 and 5. His corner strikes were a little too good. His time was coming.

"I just wasn't conditioned to pitch on three days' rest," Hurst admitted in a very quiet Red Sox locker room. "I hadn't done it all season. I knew I couldn't go the whole way. But I wanted to hold the lead."

He was through now. Carter lifted a bloop to right—caught and bobbled by a diving Dwight Evans, who nailed Hernandez at second. No matter. Wally Backman, pinch-running for Teufel, scored with the tying run.

Hurst was gone. Replaced by Calvin Schiraldi. Schiraldi? "We know about

> "Regardless of the jealousy, the envy, the hatred that exists for us, we have to be considered a great team now."
>
> —Gary Carter, Mets catcher

Mets players (from left) Rick Aguilera, Bob Ojeda, Howard Johnson, and Kevin Elster celebrate on the field at Shea Stadium after the Mets won the 1986 World Series. (Getty Images)

Schiraldi," one Met said. "We knew he didn't have any guts. We remembered him. Believe me. Guys don't change overnight."

The Mets scored three times on Schiraldi in the seventh. For all that happened afterward—Orosco's heroics in the eighth, two more Met runs in the bottom of that inning—it was Ray Knight's leadoff home run that told the Mets: the world is ours.

Knight—voted the Series MVP—said diplomatically, "Once we got into the Sox's bullpen, I knew we were in good shape. They didn't have any left-handers. They were playing right into our strength…and they all throw hard."

Hard throwers. The Mets dine on them. When Schiraldi went 2–1 on Knight, the Mets' third baseman stepped out of the box, took a deep breath, and told himself, "A fastball is coming. It's his best pitch."

It came. Knight crushed it. And in the instant the ball sailed over the left-field wall, the world did belong to the Mets. The rest was moot: two more hits, Rafael Santana's RBI single, Hernandez's sacrifice fly.

Three runs—all of which gave Orosco the cushion to bail out Roger McDowell. Evans' two-run double in the eighth made it 6–5. Orosco arrived, and admitted so much nervousness "that I was looking for the bathroom. I just told myself, 'This is no time to fold, Jesse.'"

He didn't. Rich Gedman lined out to Backman. Dave Henderson swung over four sliders. And Don Baylor bounced to short. The rally had evaporated, and so had the Red Sox.

Imagine how they felt watching Strawberry's solo homer off Al Nipper in the eighth? And Orosco's RBI single over a bunt-poised infield? The World Series was slipping away in Boston.

Schiraldi quietly called it "a very weird game. I thought we would get some good after the bad [in Game 6]. We didn't. Who can explain it? It just didn't work out for us."

Who can explain it? The Mets lost two straight at home, then took 4-of-5 from the best the American League had to offer. Champions. Say it. Champions.

Mets third baseman Ray Knight, the 1986 World Series MVP, speaks to a crowd at New York's City Hall the day after the Mets won the franchise's second World Series. Knight brought along the World Series trophy. (AP Images)

Third baseman Ray Knight (left) and catcher Gary Carter celebrate after the Mets defeated the Boston Red Sox in Game 7 of the 1986 World Series. (AP Images)

Darryl Strawberry shares a "No. 1" gesture with fans as he and his family ride through Manhattan during the ticker-tape parade the day after Mets won the 1986 World Series. (AP Images)

September 22, 1988

	123	456	789	R H E
Philadelphia Phillies	000	100	000	1 6 1
New York Mets	000	011	10X	3 9 0

Magic Moment!

AMAZIN'S TOP PHILS TO CLINCH NL EAST BY JOHN HARPER

The world didn't hate the Mets this time so much as it doubted them. Three months of mediocrity forced them to prove they had the heart and savvy to own September and win another division title.

And so this time the Mets won proud.

They won, appropriately, with pitching, as Ron Darling, smelling paydirt, gutted out the 3–1 clincher over the Phillies while Shea Stadium exploded in a dizzying wave of noise last night.

And they won with style. Last night's division clincher was their eighth straight victory and their 23rd in their last 28 games as they sprint into the playoffs.

But mostly, they won with a pride that bordered on defiance.

"To all our critics," Darryl Strawberry said, "we're still No. 1. This is a lot sweeter than '86 because we know we earned it this year. We had to work."

Maybe so, but the celebration was nothing like it was in '86, when the Mets mobbed one another on the field for what seemed like hours, while half of New York joined them. This was tame by comparison, in part because 800 cops—100 on horses—kept the fans from spilling onto the field; in part because it was the second time around.

Still, the anticipation made the final innings electric. Mookie Wilson pumped up the crowd a notch when he scored from second base on Kevin McReynolds' infield single to give the Mets a 3–1 lead in the seventh, and the roaring only built from there.

Darling wasn't about to let it get away, even pitching with a cold last night.

"I like those situations," Darling (16–9) said. "I like pitching big games."

In the eighth, with Davey Johnson forced off the bench and into his office by a stomach virus, Darling made it clear to Mel Stottlemyre how bad he wanted to finish. Back-to-back singles by Phil Bradley and Ron Jones brought Stottlemyre to the mound.

"I went out there with every intention of taking him out," Stottlemyre said. "But he had this look in his eye, and when he said, 'I can get this guy [Ricky Jordan],' I believed him."

Sure enough, Darling got an inning-ending double play; and now the crowd knew. Come the top of the ninth, the noise was deafening. Darling had goose bumps.

"Usually I can block it out," Darling said. "It's the first time I ever really felt the crowd like that. I was really pumped up. I felt like Randy Myers out there."

The ninth was one-two-three, and when Darling got Lance Parrish to strike out on a check swing at 10:09 PM, the Mets came flying out of the dugout for a hug-in at the mound.

But the celebration was brief and uneventful, as the fans stayed in their seats and cheered. In less than a minute, the Mets were off the field and headed for the clubhouse.

"The first time," Keith Hernandez said, "it had been so long since the Mets had won that there was all of that emotion. This time, it was kind of short-lived because we've done it before, and because we've got more ahead of us.

Mets fans donned blue and orange buttons in 1988 as Mets Mania caught on. The Mets won the National League East before falling to the Los Angeles Dodgers in the National League Championship Series. (Getty Images)

Mets first baseman Keith Hernandez (left) and catcher Gary Carter are all smiles as they come off the field at Shea Stadium after the Mets clinched the National League East with a 3–1 win over the Philadelphia Phillies on September 22, 1988. (AP Images)

"It will be a big one if we beat L.A. But if we don't get to the World Series, the season will be a disappointment."

Wally Backman was bolder.

"To me, it's just like '86," he said. "If we don't win it all, it won't be enough."

And Darling was bolder still.

"I'd really like to try and prove we're one of those [1972–74] Oakland A's-type teams," he said. "I've got to believe this is one of the finest teams to ever play the game."

But don't think the champagne didn't flow—and fly too—in the clubhouse. It was everywhere, players spraying it and pouring it all over anyone and everyone in the room.

It was as much a feeling of relief as triumph. As players talked about what it meant, they kept coming back to their ability to rise above their struggles in July and August.

"You don't know how many guys are looking forward to the end of the season," Howard Johnson said. "It just wasn't fun this year. It's fun now, this is great. But there was so much negative all year. I never doubted that we'd play better and get here—I'm proud of the way we came on in September—but it was really a grind."

Hernandez echoed the thoughts.

"It's just great to be back in [the playoffs]," he said. "It was a tough year for a while. The press was on us and rightly so. We played terrible. But we kept telling ourselves that the cream would rise to the top, that teams win pennants in September, and we've had a great finish. We really did rise to the occasion."

There is more work to do, but clearly, while they partied right onto a plane bound for St. Louis last night, the Mets felt like they had already proven something this season.

The Ballparks

An aerial photograph taken in April 2008 of Shea Stadium and Citi Field, under construction at the time. The Mets played their first games at new Citi Field in 2009. (Charles Wenzelberg/New York Post)

A view of the Polo Grounds shortly before the historic stadium was taken down in 1964. The Mets played their first two seasons at the former home of the New York Giants before moving into Shea Stadium in 1964. (Bob Olen/New York Post)

The Mets called three stadiums home during the team's first half century. When the National League awarded an expansion team to New York in 1960, they did so on the condition that the city build a stadium for the new club. The Mets signed a 30-year lease to play at Shea Stadium in October 1961. But the team began play in 1962, well before the new stadium in Queens could be completed.

For the team's first two seasons, the Mets called the Polo Grounds home. The stadium at West 155th Street and Eighth Avenue in northern Manhattan was home to the New York Giants from 1891 until the Giants departed for San Francisco after the 1957 season. It was also home to the Yankees from 1913 to 1922, when Yankee Stadium opened nearby in the Bronx.

The ballpark was known for its distinctive outfield. The distances down the left- and right-field lines were 279 feet and 258 feet, respectively. But the distances in the gaps were 450 feet from home plate. And straightaway center was 483 feet from the batter's box. The stadium had sat empty for more than four years, was not well maintained, and was set for demolition after the completion of the Mets' new stadium in Queens. Speaking to pitcher Tracy Stallard, who went 6–17 in 1963, Mets manager Casey Stengel told his hurler, "At the end of this season, they're gonna tear this joint down. The way you're pitchin', the right-field section will be gone already!"

The Mets moved into Shea Stadium to begin the 1964 season. The nearly 58,000-fan capacity facility was named in honor of attorney William Shea, the driving force in persuading the National League to expand and award an expansion team to New York City. The ballpark was designed to be an all-purpose park, capable of hosting both baseball and football games. The New York Jets called Shea Stadium home from 1964 through 1983. The park featured 21 escalators, 54 public rest rooms, four public restaurants and an 86 foot by 175 foot scoreboard that weighed more than 60 tons. Shea was also the first stadium to feature a "light ring." Rather than using light towers, the field was illuminated using banks of light built into the top of the facility.

In 1981, the Big Apple Top Hat was added beyond the center-field wall. The Big Apple would light up and rise out of the Top Hat following each Mets home run. Later in the 1980s, 50 suites were added to the stadium's press level and the park's exterior was painted "Mets Blue." Shea Stadium hosted the All-Star Game during its inaugural season in 1964 and was the home ballpark for both the 1969 and 1986 World Series champions.

In addition to serving as home for the Mets and Jets, the New York Yankees and the NFL's New York Giants called Shea Stadium home in 1975 during a major renovation of Yankee Stadium. Shea also hosted several memorable non-sporting events, from concerts by the Beatles and Rolling Stones to appearances by Pope John Paul II and the reverend Billy Graham. Following the September 11, 2001, attacks on New York, Shea Stadium's gates and parking areas served as a relief center.

Planning began for new ballparks for both the Yankees and Mets during the 1990s. In March 2006 the Mets revealed the model for the new ballpark. Con-

An aerial view of the Polo Grounds. The unique bathtub-shaped ballpark sat at 155th Street and Eighth Avenue in Manhattan, just across the Harlem River from Yankee Stadium in the Bronx. (AP Images)

struction began that same year, in a parking lot just beyond left field at Shea Stadium. In November 2006, it was announced that Citigroup had agreed to pay $20 million per year for 20 years for the naming rights to the park. The construction project was completed in December 2008.

Citi Field's seating capacity of 41,800 is more than 15,000 fewer than that of its predecessor, Shea. But the new ballpark offers wider seats, more legroom, significantly more wheelchair seating, more concessions and restaurants, and a larger team store. The park pays homage to New York's National League past with green seats reminiscent of the Polo Grounds and an exterior façade that bears a striking resemblance to Ebbets Field. It also carries over Shea Stadium's unique orange foul poles and the Home Run Apple—the new apple more than four times larger than the Shea Stadium version.

Citi Field's front entrance features the Jackie Robinson Rotunda, where the 160-foot diameter floor and archways feature words and images that defined the Brooklyn Dodgers' legend's life. The Mets Hall of Fame & Museum opened in April 2010 adjacent to the Jackie Robinson Rotunda. The museum features unique artifacts from the team's history, including original scouting reports on Darryl Strawberry, as well as interactive touchscreens and video displays that weave the Mets' first half century into a cohesive narrative.

The new ballpark already has carried on the Shea Stadium tradition of hosting notable non-sporting events, serving as the venue for concerts by Paul McCartney and the Dave Matthews Band.

The financing arrangement for the new ballpark included a 40-year lease for the Mets, which keeps the Mets in Queens through 2049 and assures nearly another half-century of Amazins memories for New York fans.

A view of the dedication ceremonies at Shea Stadium on April 16, 1964. The Mets played the first game at the new ballpark the next day. (Jerry Engel/New York Post)

Shea Stadium's Queens location offered a unique characteristic that differed from New York City's other baseball parks—easily accessible parking that allowed fans to drive to the game. Nonetheless, all available parking spaces were used when Shea hosted its first game on April 17, 1964. (AP Images)

Mets COO Jeff Wilpon poses in the center-field stands at Citi Field after construction was completed in December 2008.
(Charles Wenzelberg/New York Post)

Tom Seaver (right) and Mike Piazza walk toward center field during the Shea Goodbye ceremonies in September 2008. Shea Stadium was the Mets home from 1964 to 2008. (Charles Wenzelberg/New York Post)

The Citi Field sign at the new ballpark prominently features Citicorp's logo. The financial company agreed to pay $400 million over 20 years for the naming rights to the Mets' new ballpark. (AP Images)

Citi Field's design alludes to the homes of New York City's two previous National League franchises. The green seats are reminiscent of the New York Giants' Polo Grounds while the exterior façade resembles that of the Brooklyn Dodgers' Ebbets Field. (AP Images)

Greatest Games of the 1990s and 2000s

Fans use signs to express their joy at the Mets' 2000 National League championship during the NLCS-clinching win over the St. Louis Cardinals. (Getty Images)

	123	456	789	R	H	E
New York Mets	301	010	101	7	12	0
Philadelphia Phillies	000	000	000	0	3	0

Season-Ending Heat

CONE TIES NL RECORD WITH 19 STRIKEOUTS BY CHARLIE McCARTHY

David Cone made this burial one to remember.

Cone, who at 14–14 joined his teammates in not fulfilling expectations this season, yesterday tied the NL record with 19 strikeouts while three-hitting the Phillies, 7–0, in the '91 finale.

The right-hander thus joined Tom Seaver (19 Padres for Mets on April 22, 1970) and Steve Carlton (19 Mets for Cardinals on Sept. 15, 1969) as owners of the NL mark for strikeouts in a nine-inning game. Roger Clemens holds the major league mark with 20.

"It certainly gives you something to build on for the spring, and maybe it'll make the winter a little easier," Cone said, "but in no way does it make up for the season, both from a team standpoint and a personal standpoint."

Cone, who led the majors in strikeouts last year, finished with 241 to tie Clemens for that honor this season. Popular K victims at the Vet yesterday included Kim Batiste (four times), Wes Chamberlain (three), and catcher Doug Lindsey, who made his major league debut by fanning three times.

If not for the seventh, his only K-less frame, Cone would have the league record to himself. He rallied to strike out two Phillies each in the eighth and ninth. Dale Murphy grounded to short for the final out of the game to deny Cone of tying Clemens.

"It was kind of like flirting with a no-hitter," said Cone, who lost a no-no on Sept. 20 when Cardinal Felix Jose doubled with one out in the eighth.

"Nobody wanted to say anything to me. The only person that did was [Phillie coach] Larry Bowa, who said something to me after I had 15, and then again after 17. I think Bowa was excited for me, and caught up in it—at least that's the way I took it."

Reluctant to admit he once had 19 strikeouts in Little League, Cone's bid for 20 Ks actually might have disappeared in the top of the seventh, when he slightly twisted his right knee while being thrown out at the plate. Surprisingly, third-base coach Tim Spencer waved home Cone from second after Keith Miller's bloop double was kicked around in center field.

David Cone led the National League in strikeouts in 1990 and 1991. (Getty Images)

David Cone won five World Series rings after being traded from the Mets to the Toronto Blue Jays in 1992—one with Toronto and four with the New York Yankees. (Getty Images)

"I twisted my knee a little bit…I won't say it hurt me, but it stiffened up a bit," Cone said. "I was surprised a bit, especially with HoJo coming up with a chance for a couple more RBIs. I thought the ball got by the outfield, but it's tough to second guess."

Then again, '91 was a season of coulda, woulda, shoulda for the Mets, who as of 4 PM yesterday officially became GM Al Harazin's team.

Thanks to the Cubs' triumph yesterday, the Mets ended the season in fifth place, snapping a string of seven straight first- or second-place finishes. A 77–84 overall record meant a losing season for the last time since '83 (68–94), when they were managed by George Bamberger and Frank Howard.

Such dubious honors likely will precede an interesting off-season.

Expected free agents like Bobby Bonilla, Steve Buechele, and Glenn Davis should interest Harazin, and then there's free-agent-to-be Frank Viola, who yesterday bolted before all his teammates had reached the clubhouse.

"I wanted to leave after the sixth inning," Viola admitted while exiting, "but Conie had 15 strikeouts. I said, 'I'm not leaving this.'"

At the top of Harazin's list will be naming a manager, who could be Jeff Torborg, Dallas Green, or incumbent Mike Cubbage.

"I'm going to make some calls; Al said he would stay in touch with me," Cubbage said. "Al said he did not have a timetable."

Cubbage, who directed a 3–7 ending after replacing Bud Harrelson, apparently has the backing of many players.

Howard Johnson gave Cubbage a souvenir bat with "38 HRs, 117 RBIs, 30 SBs" inscribed on it; and, as the press filed into the manager's office, Daryl Boston yelled only half-jokingly: "Tell them to sign [Cubbage] or I'm out of here."

> "Nobody wanted to say anything to me. The only person that did was [Phillie coach] Larry Bowa, who said something to me after I had 15, and then again after 17. I think Bowa was excited for me, and caught up in it— at least that's the way I took it."
>
> —David Cone

	1 2 3	4 5 6	7 8 9	R H E
Montreal Expos	0 0 0	0 1 0	0 1 0	2 7 2
New York Mets	0 0 1	0 1 1	0 0 X	3 7 2

Franco Gets 300th Save

LEFTY REACHES MILESTONE MARK BY RAY MCNULTY

Pete Harnisch allowed only three hits and one unearned run against the best-hitting team in the major leagues in what easily was his best pitching performance since July.

Rey Ordonez went 2-for-3 to extend his National League–best hitting streak to 14 games and raise his batting average to a whopping .354.

And the Mets, with a hard-fought, well-deserved, 3–2 victory over the first-place Expos, left Shea with their first three-game winning streak of the season.

But last night belonged to John Franco, who waited through a 100-minute rain delay and eight fog-shrouded innings for his chance to make baseball history, to earn his 300th career save, to make his bid for the Hall of Fame.

All of which he did in a ninth inning he'll never forget, exactly 12 years to the day he picked up his first big-league save.

It began with Darren Fletcher looking at a called third strike. Then came an infield single by F.P. Santangelo, who went to second when third baseman Jeff Kent's hurried, off-balance throw bounced into the seats.

Suddenly, two outs from a milestone with the tying run in scoring position, Franco's memorable moment was in jeopardy. But after striking out Shane Andrews, the Brooklyn-born Met closer got the final out when pinch-hitter Sherman Obando flied to center field.

It was 12:11 AM. The game was history. And so was Franco, who became only the eighth reliever—and the first left-hander—to reach the 300-save plateau.

"I guess that means I've had a pretty damn good career so far," said Franco, 35, who is tied with Bruce Sutter for seventh on the all-time save list. "Especially for someone who wasn't supposed to make it in the big leagues.

"Really, I'm pretty choked up about it. I wish my parents were around for this. I'm just glad I got it here at home."

Unfortunately, most of the crowd of 14,011 either had left during the rain delay or didn't bother to stay past midnight to witness Franco's heroics.

John Franco pitches against the Montreal Expos on April 29, 1996, en route to his 300th career save. Franco became the first left-handed pitcher to reach 300 saves. (AP Images)

John Franco celebrates in the arms of Mets first baseman Rico Brogna after collecting his 300th career save. Franco pitched the ninth inning, striking out two Montreal Expos for his fifth save of the season. (AP Images)

But Franco's teammates knew how much this night meant to their club-house leader.

Just as center fielder Lance Johnson grabbed the final out, first baseman Rico Brogna rushed over to Franco and lifted him off the soggy infield. And within seconds, the entire Met team was mobbing the veteran left-hander.

"I was thinking about it because I definitely wanted to be the guy he got the save for," Harnisch said. "And I knew this would be the only chance I'd get because, five days from now, he'd probably already have gotten it.

"This was a big night for us…for a lot of reasons."

The Mets, after all, began the night six games behind the front-running Expos in the NL East. And they see this three-game series as a measuring stick.

So to score three runs against Jeff Fassero and hold the Expos to only two runs—Montreal scored 21 Sunday against the Rockies—was significant. Even if it is only April.

"This was a great night for our ballclub," Met manager Dallas Green said. "We wanted to show well against Montreal, and tonight was an example of how we can play when we put all of the ingredients together. This gives us a tremendous lift."

The Mets pushed across runs in the second, fifth, and sixth innings on doubles by Ordonez, Edgardo Alfonzo, and Kent. And Harnisch and Franco made those runs stand up.

Harnisch, in fact, allowed only three singles and three walks, and he struck out five. The one run he allowed was the result of his own sixth-inning throwing error, an errant pickoff attempt at second, which was the only time the ball left the infield in the inning.

"This was the most life I've had in my fastball since before the shoulder surgery," Harnisch said, referring to his season-ending August operation. "It's been a while since I felt that good out there."

It's been a while since the Mets, as a team, felt this good about the way they're playing baseball. And this win belonged to all of them—but none more than Franco.

"Johnny got his 300th, and there couldn't have been a tougher one in the bunch," Green said. "This was a great No. 300. He won't forget that one for a while."

> **"This was a great No. 300. He won't forget that one for a while."**
>
> **—Dallas Green, Mets manager**

October 4, 1999

	1 2 3	4 5 6	7 8 9	R H E
New York Mets	2 0 1	0 1 1	0 0 0	5 9 0
Cincinnati Reds	0 0 0	0 0 0	0 0 0	0 2 0

Al-Elujah!

LEITER'S A LATTER-DAY KOOZ BY TOM KEEGAN

Sopping wet from champagne, holding a bottle in his right hand, sharing a bear hug with another kid who grew up pulling for the Mets, Al Leiter had the most poignant words of the evening aimed right down his bubbly-lubricated throat.

"Jerry Koosman! Jerry Koosman! Jerry Koosman!" Shawon Dunston kept hollering until Leiter slogged his way to the next hug, the next attaboy, the next blast of champagne thank yous.

Leiter is indeed the Jerry Koosman of his generation. From out of a season even he termed "mediocre" an already considerable reputation as a big-game pitcher grew and grew and grew.

The Mets so desperately needed a win back in June when their losing streak stood at eight games and a pregame news conference in the Bronx was held to announce the firing of three coaches. Yankee logos were spread all over the country thanks to the Mets.

But that evening belonged to the Mets because Leiter stuck it to the Yankees. He turned their season around.

As badly as the Mets needed that one, they needed a win even worse last week at Shea Stadium with the Braves in town. The Mets' losing streak swelled to seven games. Five of those were pinned on them by the Braves.

Leiter rode to the rescue again, reversed the fortunes of the Mets again.

And then there was last night, the Mets' biggest game in more than a decade. Leiter was better than ever, more locked in on catcher Mike Piazza's mitt, more passionate about every pitch, every at-bat, every inning.

He was Mario Cuomo giving the best speech of his life. Michael Jordan on fire. Robert DeNiro immersed in his character.

He was Jerry Koosman three decades later.

He was an ace.

Mets pitcher Al Leiter raises his arms in celebration after the Mets defeated the Cincinnati Reds in a one-game playoff to determine the National League wild card winner in 1999. Leiter gave up just two hits in the complete game shutout. (Getty Images)

132

Third baseman Robin Ventura hoists teammate Masato Yoshii into the air as Bobby Bonilla looks on after the Mets defeated the Cincinnati Reds to win the National League wild card. (Nury Hernandez/New York Post)

It took last night's two-hit shutout in a 5–0 win over the Reds in a one-game playoff that earned the Mets the National League wild card for Leiter (13–12) to finish the regular season with a record better than .500.

Sometimes it's not the number of wins as much as it's the size of them.

The Yankees win was big. The Braves win was bigger. The Reds win was the biggest of the year, but not of his career. He did not get the win but was the starting pitcher for the Marlins in their 1997 Game 7 victory over the Indians.

This was his best big-game performance. Jeffrey Hammonds lined a sharp single to left in the second and Pokey Reese doubled down the left-field line in the ninth. In between, Leiter no-hit the Reds.

It's nights like these that can get a guy elected senator of New Jersey down the road.

Two-hit shutouts went out with bell-bottom sideburns, turtleneck sweaters, *The Partridge Family*.

This is the age of set-up men and closers and strike zones the size of needle eyes and juiced baseballs and steroid-inflated hitters and pitch counts.

Big-game pitchers transcend the conditions of the time. Turn up the lights and watch them put on a show.

Leiter wasn't a better pitcher this year than last, but he had a better year.

He went 17–6 with a 2.47 ERA in 1998 and placed sixth in the Cy Young Award voting. He won't get a Cy Young vote this time, but the trophy case that resides in his memory banks is packed with big moments and more could be on the horizon.

"I'll take a mediocre year anytime if I can get to the playoffs," Leiter said. "Of course, I'd like to be standing here with 20 wins, but I could have fallen apart, I could have crumbled with all the things that happened, but I didn't do that."

He could have crumbled, he could have fallen apart six pitches, all balls, into the game. This was no way to treat a 2–0 lead bestowed upon him by Edgardo Alfonzo's two-run home run. Mike Piazza paid him a visit on the mound, triggering stadium-shaking boos from the 54,621 who came to witness a season in a night.

Leiter found it immediately after that noisy little break and never lost it. From the time Leiter walked Barry Larkin with two outs in the third to the leadoff walk to Eddie Taubensee in the eighth, Leiter retired 13 in a row, a stretch that secured his 13th win and put the Mets in the postseason.

The Reds didn't advance a runner past first until Reese doubled and took third in the ninth.

Leiter pitched the entire night with leads. The biggest out?

"The last one," Leiter said. "I really wanted to be out there celebrating as one of the nine on the field, as opposed to other times I've done it when I had to run from the dugout or somewhere else to join the celebration."

With runners on the corners, Dmitri Young lined to Alfonzo for the final out. Corks popped. Champagne flew. A reputation was cemented.

	1 2 3	4 5 6	7 8 9	10	R H E
Arizona Diamondbacks	0 0 0	0 1 0	0 2 0	0	3 5 1
New York Mets	0 0 0	1 0 1	0 1 0	1	4 8 0

The Journeyman Arrives

NO-NAME PRATT NOW N.Y. HERO BY WALLACE MATTHEWS

Time stopped at 4:33 yesterday afternoon at a ballpark in Flushing, the precise moment Steve Finley began his climb toward the top of the center-field fence, Todd Pratt halted his trip around the bases and 56,177 people held a collective breath.

Pratt already was well into his customary home-run trot, the one that ends with a half-circle back to the dugout after 120 feet, when his teammates began celebrating what he had yet to realize.

After all, his six-year major league career had been a series of letdowns, send-downs, and pass-overs.

In 11 minor league seasons, he had managed all of 77 home runs, and had hit only 16 in the majors.

Why should he for one instant believe that Steve Finley wouldn't come down with that baseball, that this game, the biggest he had ever played in, wouldn't grind on to yet another bad ending for the Mets, and that one more time, Todd Pratt would wind up being not quite good enough?

Yesterday, Todd Pratt was finally good enough.

When that ball finally came down, time did more than stop at Shea Stadium.

It rolled backward, to celebrated Octobers gone by, to the games in which Bobby Thomson and Bucky Dent and Jim Leyritz found themselves in the same spot that Pratt did yesterday, staring out at an outfielder and hoping he would come down with his glove empty.

"I saw Steve starting to plant for his jump and we've all seen it a million times on the highlight films, Steve bringing back balls," Pratt said. "I didn't know if he had it. I couldn't see the ball."

The next time Pratt saw the baseball, it was being handed to him outside the Met clubhouse by Charlie Rappa, a fireworks technician whose job it was to set off the pyrotechnics in the event the home team won the game.

At 4:33, Charlie Rappa retrieved the baseball, lit the fuse, and Shea Stadium exploded.

Todd Pratt, thrust into the most thankless role any Met could be assigned—filling the shoes of the injured Mike Piazza—hit a home run that may someday be remembered the

way Leyritz's is, the way Dent's is, the way Thomson's is, nearly 50 years after it was hit.

"Honestly, I just don't think it's that big a deal," said Pratt, his voice hoarse from shouting, his hair and body soaked in cheap celebratory champagne. "To be honest with you, it was just another game."

Pratt played his moment in the sun as if he expected that someday Gary Cooper will play him in the movie. He came to the moment the way heroes are supposed to come, soft-spoken and modest and even a bit embarrassed by all the attention.

"I am going to kiss my wife, give my son a high-five, and then probably, I will be back on my computer playing computer games," he said. "Hey, I could have easily been the goat today."

Instead, Todd Pratt turned out to be the kind of hero we remember around here for a long, long time.

Pratt's shot to dead center field, which came to earth 414 feet from home plate in the bottom of the 10th inning of an excruciating, electrifying ballgame, put the Mets into the National League Championship Series, just four wins from the World Series.

It came off Matt Mantei, the Arizona Diamondback closer who probably should have pitched an inning in Game 1 but wound up pitching two yesterday, and with the game deadlocked at 3 and the Diamondbacks' future at stake, manager Buck Showalter asked him for one more.

Mantei made it three pitches into the inning when Pratt got hold of a fastball—Mantei had hit 97 mph striking out Rey Ordonez to end the eighth—and sent it to the deepest part of the ballpark.

He and Finley took off at a dead run at precisely the same time, but rounding first, Pratt stopped to see whether any further effort was necessary. "When you see Steve go back on a ball slow like that, it usually means he's timing it," said Darryl Hamilton, a pretty good center fielder in his own right. "When I saw him go up," Pratt said, "My heart stopped."

Seconds later, Todd Pratt's life began. At 32 years old, with a baseball lifetime of disappointments behind him, finally he had done something that will get him free drinks for the rest of his life.

In his six abortive big-league seasons, Todd Pratt had seen chance after chance come and go by. Always, there was hope, and always, it seemed, someone better than he came along to dash it.

He had toiled as a backup to Todd Hundley, an iron man before he blew out his elbow, and then found his position as Hundley's successor challenged and ultimately usurped by the likes of Tim Spehr and Alberto Castillo and Jorge Fabregas and Rick Wilkins.

When he got sent down at the start of last season, Pratt remained in his apartment for three miserable days, paralyzed with despair, until Rick Dempsey, Bobby Valentine's successor as the manager of the Triple-A Norfolk Mets, talked him out of giving it all up to manage a pizza parlor.

Teammates mob Todd Pratt at home plate after Pratt hit a game-winning home run in the tenth inning of Game 4 to clinch the National League Division Series. (Getty Images)

"Last year was a very heartbreaking year for me," Pratt said. "I hated baseball at that point because I knew I was too good a player and was just getting a bad rap. They just didn't think I was good enough. Every time I got sent down, I didn't deserve it. I mean, everybody makes a big deal out of Mike Piazza here, which is correct, but I'm the Mike Piazza of Triple A."

Not quite, but yesterday, Todd Pratt was the closest thing to Mike Piazza the Mets could scare up. With their $91 million catcher laid up with a bad thumb, it was up to Pratt to fill the void behind the plate, if not in the lineup.

And two innings earlier, Pratt had been on the back end of a play that saved the game for the Mets, taking a throw from left fielder Melvin Mora and slapping a tag on Jay Bell as he attempted to score what would have been the Diamondbacks' fourth run.

"Without that throw by Melvin Mora and without the pitching performance that Al Leiter gave us, I wouldn't have had the chance to do what I did," Pratt said. "I had had some chances [he grounded out twice with runners in scoring position] earlier and didn't come through. Hey, I know I'm not the offensive force Mike is, but I can handle the bat all right."

Batting against Mantei in the eighth, the 6-foot-3, 230-pound Pratt had choked up on the bat to deal with the heat, and managed only a ground-out to third.

"The second time up, I told myself, 'I'm not choking up this time,'" Pratt said. "The first pitch was a curve that wasn't even close and I thought if it's a

fastball anywhere I can touch it, I'm swinging. He actually threw it just where I like it, a little up and out over the plate."

Pratt liked it so much he gave it a ride, but he wasn't sure how much of a ride until the sight of his teammates, in full charge out of the dugout, persuaded him that for once, he was running the wrong way.

"I turned back and saw Steve put his head down," Todd Pratt said. "That's when I finally knew it was out."

Time stopped, the game ended, the Mets' improbable thrill ride of a season continued.

And Todd Pratt's life as a New York baseball hero began.

> "I saw Steve [Finley] starting to plant for his jump and we've all seen it a million times on the highlight films, Steve bringing back balls, I didn't know if he had it. I couldn't see the ball."
>
> —Todd Pratt, Mets catcher

March 30, 2000

	1 2 3	4 5 6	7 8 9	10 11	R H E
New York Mets	000	010	000	0 4	5 6 2
Chicago Cubs	000	010	000	0 0	1 5 0

Benny's Shot Heard 'Round the World

SLAM IN 11ᵀᴴ EARNS METS SPLIT BY ANDREW MARCHAND

Too bad Bobby Valentine can't write 26 guys on his lineup card.

How fitting was it? How fitting was it—that with the international incident over Don Baylor's possible use of an extra man on Opening Day hanging over Game 2 of the season—that Benny Agbayani, the Mets' 26ᵗʰ man, came through?

It was very fitting because these are the 2000 Mets. Get used to them, because the only thing we know for sure is that drama and intrigue will be a part of every day with these Mets.

So with the score tied at one in the 11ᵗʰ inning and the bases loaded with two outs, Agbayani, a native Hawaiian who grew up closest to Japan of any Met, stepped to the plate.

It was the same Agbayani who is scheduled to be sent down on April 9 when No. 5 starter Glendon Rusch is recalled to pitch against the Dodgers at Shea.

It was the same 28-year-old Agbayani who is the victim of the numbers games that did not allow for a fair competition this spring between him and his best friend, Jay Payton, who is out of minor league options, for the right-handed hitting outfield spot off the bench.

So Agbayani—who because of the circumstances requested a trade this spring—faced rookie lefty Danny Young.

Now, realize if the Mets had lost, they would have had a 12½-hour plane ride back to New York, followed by two off days until the home opener Monday to deal with losing two games to the expected to be abysmal Cubs. Plus, there would be all of the bad vibes piled on by the unrelenting comments made by Baylor about Valentine.

"0–2 would have been tough," said GM Steve Phillips, who is responsible for the Agbayani decision.

So, of course, Agbayani came through, hitting a 1–0 pitch just over the center-field wall to give the Mets the 5–1 win over the Cubs in 11 innings at the sold-out Tokyo Dome here.

"I really don't know what pitch I hit," Agbayani said. "It was low where I like it and I just hit it out."

Does it change anything for April 9ᵗʰ?

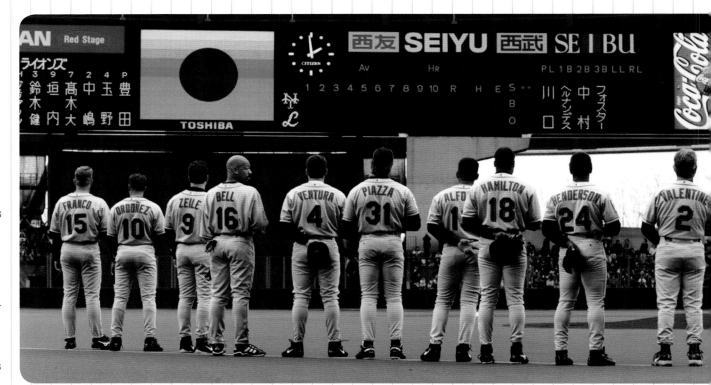

Mets players line up on the Seibu Dome field after introductions to listen to the Japanese national anthem on March 26, 2000. The Mets defeated the Seibu Lions 8–1 in an exhibition game in preparation for their season-opening series against the Cubs in Tokyo. (Getty Images)

Mets catcher Mike Piazza and manager Bobby Valentine are greeted by ceremonial kimono ladies before taking on the Chicago Cubs in the season opener on March 29, 2000. (Getty Images)

"Not at this point it doesn't," said Phillips, who added things are subject to change.

Unless you're talking about major league baseball in Japan. The second game of the Japan series still didn't have that beginning of the summer feel. The abundantly polite Japanese didn't get as into it as major leaguers are used to.

That is until Valentine strategically walked Sammy Sosa in the 10th with two out and a man on second. This prompted much of the crowd to rise from their seats and put their thumbs down and boo.

"I thought it would take more than four days back in Japan for the fans to boo me," kidded Valentine, who managed Chiba Lotte in '95 here.

Dennis Cook replaced Turk Wendell on the mound to go up against lefty Mark Grace. Cook pitched around him and walked Grace on four pitches. So the bases were loaded for Henry Rodriguez. Cook struck him out swinging. This set up Agbayani.

What gets lost in Agbayani's night was the splendid pitching of Rick Reed. Reed threw eight innings of four-hit ball and only gave up an un-earned run because new first baseman Todd Zeile made a throwing error in the bottom of the fifth.

The victory covers up scrutiny about this play and Zeile's ability at first. It covers up the talk about the right-handed lineup as well.

Two games is not a sample to draw conclusions, but it is the beginning of one. The predominance of right-handed hitters in the lineup will bring focus when a guys like Jon Lieber and Kyle Farnsworth (5–9, 5.09 ERA last season), who threw 5⅔ innings of three-hit, one-run ball in Game 2.

It will start new talk though. Should Agbayani be on the team?

This will get even more interesting. The next batter up, Payton, hit a double to right.

> ## "I thought it would take more than four days back in Japan for the fans to boo me..."
>
> **—Bobby Valentine, Mets manager**

September 27, 2000

	1 2 3	4 5 6	7 8 9	R H E
Atlanta Braves	1 0 0	0 0 0	0 0 1	2 6 1
New York Mets	0 0 0	1 3 1	1 0 X	6 9 1

It's Amazin'!

METS WILD BUNCH AGAIN BY GEORGE WILLIS

Mike Piazza, the symbol of the Mets' three-year rise from division laughingstock to postseason participant, stood in the middle of a champagne-soaked clubhouse and offered no apologies for being the NL wild-card team for the second straight year.

"Through the year we never stopped growing and learning," Piazza said, while champagne dripped from his sleeve. "Going through the hard times makes this time so good."

A 6–2 victory over the Braves last night at Shea allowed the Mets a chance to celebrate. For the first time in franchise history, they have earned back-to-back trips to the postseason. That it came as a wild-card again may disappoint those who have grown weary of finishing second to the Braves. But the Mets weren't about to act like this was some sort of consolation prize.

"Come Sunday, there will be 22 teams going home," said John Franco, who waited 16 years before reaching the postseason last year. "We'll still be playing. That's an accomplishment in itself. Once you're in, anything can happen."

Certainly, the Diamondbacks would like to be where the Mets are. So would the Dodgers and even the Indians. But it's the Mets who earned the right to keep playing. So they celebrated last night, dousing each other with hugs and alcohol, trying to feel as good as the Braves did Tuesday night when they partied in the clubhouse down the hall after clinching the NL East.

"This is a good time for some guys who have worked hard," Bobby Valentine said. "It's a chance for them to catch a deep breath."

While the music was loud and festive in the clubhouse, there was a feeling of ambivalence in the stadium as if this trip to the postseason is some kind of death march. Amid the crowd of 48,858 there were encouraging signs like: "You Gotta Believe," but after being beaten up by the Braves for most of the year, some might question, "Why bother?"

Recent history tells us that should the Mets somehow get past the Giants or the Cardinals in the division series, they'll only be subjected to another humbling loss to the Braves in the NLCS. Perhaps that's why many in the stands weren't as joyous as the

Mets closer Armando Benitez pumps his fist after striking out Atlanta's Keith Lockhart for the final out. The Mets secured their second straight National League wild card with the 6–2 win over the Braves. (Getty Images)

Timo Perez slides into third base on this fifth-inning triple. Perez scored to give the Mets a 2–1 lead when the next batter, Darryl Hamilton, singled him home. (AP Images)

players. In fact, about half the crowd was gone by the time Armando Benitez struck out Keith Lockhart for the final out.

There were no mounted police lining the field. No fireworks. No drama. It took an announcement over the public address that the Mets had clinched the wild-card to draw a hearty ovation.

The players, meanwhile, sauntered onto the field to congratulate each other much like any other victory. There was no pile-up on the mound. No tears. It wasn't until they got back in the clubhouse and saw the free booze that they went nuts.

"Everybody should enjoy this," Piazza said. "We've worked hard."

Had the Mets been playing anyone other than the Braves last night, clinching a wild-card might have been a more joyous occasion for all concerned. But the Braves' mastery of the Mets this year put the home team in the uncomfortable position of defending this postseason berth.

Before last night's game, Valentine was quizzed on how much celebrating his team should do once it qualified to play in October. The insinuation was that the Mets deserved to celebrate a little, but not too much. After all, they couldn't beat the Braves to win the division.

Such notions test the patience of Valentine.

"After 158 games, that another team has three more wins in our league than we do, they should be able to feel better about themselves at this time

of the year than we do? I just don't get it," Valentine said.

"St. Louis has won one more game in every 50 than we have," he added. "And they're supposed to feel like the king, and in our city, people think that we should run away and hide and be embarrassed about entering the play-offs. I don't get it and neither do my guys."

Piazza certainly wasn't apologizing. Nor was he counting the Mets out of the 2000 World Series. "There's another season coming up," he said. "Hope-fully, we'll be the team that wins the last game of the year."

The only people who really believe that might happen wear METS across their chests. The Braves, Giants, and Cardinals go into the postseason with more momentum than the September-challenged Mets.

But miracles do happen in sports. The Jets beat the Colts in Super Bowl III; America's 1980 hockey team beat the Russians en route to the gold medal; Villanova upset Georgetown in 1985 for the NCAA title. Just yesterday, the U.S.A. baseball team beat the Cubans for the gold in Sydney.

Maybe the Mets can beat the Braves? Who knows, maybe Robin Ventura can break out of a season-long slump and be a postseason hero. Maybe Piazza might carry the team with his bat. Maybe the Mets can play like they did in August instead of September. Quit laughing.

The Mets wore their NL wild-card hats proudly last night. They've won 90 games and a second straight trip to the playoffs. No apologies necessary.

	1 2 3	4 5 6	7 8 9	R H E
St. Louis Cardinals	0 0 0	0 0 0	0 0 0	0 3 2
New York Mets	3 0 0	3 0 0	1 0 X	7 10 0

Bring On the Yanks

METS TOP CARDINALS, ADVANCE TO SUBWAY SERIES BY ANDREW MARCHAND

The 44-year-old dream is here and GM Steve Phillips echoed the thoughts of co-owner Fred Wilpon. He was rooting for the guys with the pinstripes in the ALCS.

"I am happy it is the Yankees," Phillips said in a teleconference early this morning after the Yankees clinched the ALCS and guaranteed a Subway Series.

"I think it is extremely good for baseball and the city of New York and it is another historical event."

The Yankees—who will open at home Saturday—won four of the six games between the teams this season, which, of course, was really turned into a rivalry when Roger Clemens conked Mike Piazza on his head. This series can't be over-hyped enough: it is the biggest of any of the players' lives.

"This is for all the marbles," Phillips said. "The stakes are certainly much higher now. You turn on that emotion exponentially."

The top of the Mets' staff matched up very well with the Yankees this season. Mike Hampton in his one start, on three days' rest, pitched seven innings of shutout baseball. Al Leiter went twice against the Yankees and split his two decisions, but his ERA was just 2.40.

While Rick Reed didn't pitch against the Yankees, Bobby Jones made two starts against the Bronx Bombers and he wasn't even close to perfect. Jones was 0–2 with a 7.71 ERA and started those games.

The cost of a subway ride in '56 was 15 cents compared to $1.50 today, so things are different today. Plus, the teams met in the regular season, not like in the old days.

But in these players' careers they will never play another series as big as this one.

"Only Subway II would be as big, maybe bigger or Subway Series III," Phillips said. "Getting to the World Series for most of us is the pinnacle of our careers."

Mets pitcher Mike Hampton and catcher Mike Piazza celebrate after Hampton recorded the final out of Game 5 of the National League Championship Series. Hampton was the MVP of the series, throwing seven scoreless innings in Game 1 and a complete game shutout in Game 5. (Getty Images)

Fans celebrate in the stands during the Mets' 7–0 win over the St. Louis Cardinals to clinch the National League pennant. (Getty Images)

Such a pinnacle that Phillips slept until 1 PM yesterday for the first time in his life, he said, as he was tired from the late-night celebration that lasted into yesterday morning.

The series will bring a new playoff challenge for the Mets as in Yankee Stadium, there will be a DH, which figures to be Piazza with Todd Pratt catching or lefties Darryl Hamilton or Lenny Harris with Piazza behind the plate. A guy like Harris could be a major factor in this series.

A lot of people will be talking about May 22, 1998, and December 23, 1999, and rightfully so, because those are the respective dates Phillips brought in the Mighty Mikes—Piazza and Hampton. But don't forget the smaller dates like June 2, 2000.

That is the date the Mets gave up Bill Pulsipher to the Diamondbacks for Harris and some cash. No matter how cliche it is to say: it takes 25 guys to win a championship.

Harris is the leader of a group of unsung Mets, which includes names like reliever Rick White, backup catcher Todd Pratt, utilityman Joe McEwing, pinch-hitter Bubba Trammell, infielders Matt Franco and Kurt Abbott, and a guy like Pat Mahomes, who hasn't even been on the playoff roster.

But the acquisition of Harris brought an energy to the clubhouse that wasn't as potent beforehand. He came with a message for the younger players.

"I kind of get the young guys together and say, 'We can do this. You never know if you are going to get this opportunity again,'" Harris said. "So it was a big plus. So it was a big plus with Timo [Perez,] [Jay] Payton, and [Benny] Agbayani to come through, I said, 'Hey, don't wait for Mike Piazza to hit the three-run bomb all the time, but play like you are capable of playing and do the things you are capable of doing and we can go a long way.' And those guys answered. They really answered."

The burly-looking Harris, from Miami, has no trouble expressing himself. He is smooth with his words and able to crack a joke with the lethal quickness of Dan Marino's release.

He is not the only one who was unmistakably ecstatic about his first World Series. White, brought over with Trammell on July 28 from Tampa, went over to Phillips and put his arm around him and said, "Thank you."

> "Getting to the World Series for most of us is the pinnacle of our careers."
>
> —Steve Phillips, Mets general manager

The Mets' Mike Hampton and Edgardo Alfonzo react dejectedly in the dugout as the Yankees finished off their 2000 World Series win with a Game 5 victory at Shea Stadium. (Charles Wenzelberg/New York Post)

Mike Piazza reacts after Roger Clemens threw his broken bat at him as Piazza headed toward first base in Game 2 of the 2000 World Series. (Nury Hernandez/New York Post)

	123	456	789	R H E
San Francisco Giants	010	010	000	2 6 1
New York Mets	110	000	06X	8 11 1

Piazza Stands Alone

HR SETS CATCHER MARK AS METS SMASH GIANTS BY MICHAEL MORRISSEY

History had just been made, and Mike Piazza rejoined his teammates in the Mets' dugout with a smile wider than Manhattan. You could tell how much the record meant to him, and you could sense the weight lifted from his shoulders.

With two outs in the first inning last night, Piazza officially established himself as the greatest all-time power-hitting catcher. He broke his tie with Carlton Fisk, smashing his 352nd career homer as a catcher to right-center off Giants righty Jerome Williams.

There was plenty to celebrate for Mets fans, because Shane Spencer hit a tie-breaking, two-out, three-run homer in the eighth and Mike Cameron followed with a two-run jack to help secure an 8–2, rain-delayed victory.

"What can I say? I'm obviously very proud," Piazza said. "I'm excited. I'm a little bit relieved."

The Mets (12–15) used clutch two-out hitting and 4⅔ innings of unhittable relief to secure their third straight victory, but it all took a back seat to the end of Piazza's quest.

"It was a great feeling…and he pulverized it," Art Howe said. "That ball was scorched."

Piazza hit his record-book homer in signature fashion—working the count to 3-and-1 before utilizing his tremendous opposite-field power. It was a no-doubt clout that measured 405 feet and bounced off the base of the scoreboard. Piazza briefly watched the trajectory before embarking on his record-setting HR trot.

"I felt like I had a monkey jump off my back," a grinning Piazza said of his trip around the bases.

As he touched home, he did something he never does—he pointed skyward.

"My faith is very important to me," he said. "I've lived a dream and I've worked hard of course. I'm truly blessed in my life."

His teammates waited for him near the top step of the dugout, and Piazza broke out in an irrepressible smile as he received congratulations. He answered a raucous curtain call

Mike Piazza rounds the bases after hitting his 352nd career home run as a catcher, breaking Carlton Fisk's major league record. (Nury Hernandez/New York Post)

144

Baseball's greatest power-hitting catchers honor Mike Piazza's record before an interleague game against the Detroit Tigers on June 18, 2004. Pictured from left are Gary Carter, Johnny Bench, Carlton Fisk, Piazza, Yogi Berra, and Ivan Rodriguez. (AP Images)

from the crowd of 19,974, holding his helmet high in his right hand and waving to the Shea faithful.

Then he did what he's proudly done nearly his entire professional career—he began donning his catcher's gear and preparing for the next half-inning.

But not before he uttered a joke to Howe.

"I said, 'Now get me to first base. I'm tired of catching,'" Piazza said.

The record has been a long time coming, and the team cornerstone was miffed by the Mets' ham-handed attempts to move him to first base.

He went his final 88 at-bats of last season and the first at-bat this season without a homer, the longest stretch in his career. He suffered his second-longest homerless spell—64 at-bats—before he hit his fourth homer of the year in Los Angeles on April 27 to tie Fisk's record.

Despite Piazza's blast, the Mets couldn't put away the Giants—who were without their own record-setting slugger as Barry Bonds missed his second straight game with a sinus infection.

> ## "I said, 'Now get me to first base. I'm tired of catching.'"
> —Mike Piazza, Mets catcher

The two teams were deadlocked at 2–2 after five innings when torrential rains began, causing a one-hour, 19-minute delay.

In the eighth, Piazza nearly padded his record and broke the tie. He crushed a full-count pitch from fireballing reliever Felix Rodriguez deep to center, but the ball died at the track to the left of the 410-foot mark.

But the Mets sandwiched singles by Todd Zeile and Karim Garcia around Piazza's near-miss, and Spencer greeted reliever Matt Herges with a 405-foot jack to center. Cameron followed with a two-run homer into the outfield bleachers.

	123	456	789	RHE
Florida Marlins	000	000	000	042
New York Mets	002	011	00X	480

Mets Livin' In Crown Town

WAIT OVER AS AMAZINS CLINCH NL EAST BY MARK HALE

Billy Wagner and Paul Lo Duca hugged on the field. The mob of Mets formed on the infield, players running in from the bullpen and the team hugging and supplying congratulations.

Fireworks went up, as the Mets' fifth NL East title is official.

The Shea scoreboard shouted, THE TEAM. THE TIME. THE 2006 NL EAST CHAMPS. The Mets finally did it last night, clinching their fifth NL East title and first since 1988 with a 4–0 victory over the Marlins in front of 46,729 at Shea.

The Mets had missed out on clinching the division by falling in all three games at PNC Park in Pittsburgh over the weekend, while the Phillies won all three of their contests in Houston.

But last night, Steve Trachsel, who turns 36 next month and who has never appeared in a playoff game, was phenomenal as he scattered three hits through six shutout innings. He had been horrible in his previous two starts, but saved his best for when the Mets needed him most.

Meanwhile, Jose Valentin drove in the first three runs for the Mets, slamming a pair of homers.

Before the game, there was plastic covering several TVs in the center of the Mets clubhouse. In the hallway outside, there were four carts of champagne bottles. After Trachsel retired the Marlins in order in the third, Genesis' "Tonight, Tonight, Tonight" played on the loudspeaker, a fitting song.

Valentin, who came into the game in a 5-for-36 slump, hit his first homer in the bottom of the third after Shawn Green was hit by a pitch in his fourth straight game. Valentin then slammed an 0–1 pitch 395 feet into the back of the right field bullpen for a 2–0 Mets lead.

Two innings later, the second baseman ripped his second homer to right, this one traveling 405 feet.

In the sixth, Carlos Beltran walked to lead off, and after Carlos Delgado struck out, David Wright reached on a Miguel Cabrera error at third. Cliff Floyd then made it 4–0, grounding an RBI single to right.

Jose Valentin points after crossing the plate following his solo home run in the fifth inning. Valentin's blast gave the Mets a 3–0 lead. (AP Images)

Closer Billy Wagner reacts after recording the final out of the Mets' 4–0 win over the Florida Marlins to clinch the National League East title. (AP Images)

Trachsel didn't surrender a hit through the first 3⅔ innings, issuing only a walk to Cabrera in the first. In the fourth, Josh Willingham drove a two-out double to left-center, but Trachsel caught Mike Jacobs looking to end the inning. Trachsel struck out three Marlins last night, walking one.

Trachsel had made 28 previous starts this season, and hadn't pitched a scoreless outing in any of them. Last night, though, he left the game to a huge ovation in the seventh inning.

Trachsel had permitted only one hit in the first six innings, and after he gave up two singles in the seventh with one out, Guillermo Mota got Cody Ross on a pop-up and Alfredo Amezaga on a fly to left.

The Mets scored a total of five runs in their three games in Pittsburgh over the weekend, and Valentin's homers accounted for their only runs in the first five innings.

Valentin's third-inning homer was the Mets' first hit last night, and when Reyes later singled in the inning, he was caught stealing third. In the fourth, Beltran led off with a double to center, but after Delgado advanced him to third with a ground-out, Wright popped out and Floyd whiffed.

The '86 Mets on the '06 Mets

"It's amazing. Twenty years since '86 and 18 since winning the division. Talk about some mileage, bro. I go to New York every year and every time someone talks about the '86 Mets. Every time. I'm so happy for the fans. No matter what anybody says, New York has the best sports fans in the world."

—Lenny Dykstra

"They've got a lot of pizzazz to them, a lot of class. You don't see anyone loafing. They're always out there busting their butts. They play the game like it's the last one on Earth."

—Kevin Mitchell

"To me, all the places I played, there's no greater place to be in the situation they are, where they're going to the playoffs, than New York. The fans were great to us and I'm sure they'll be great to them."

—Wally Backman

October 7, 2006

	123	456	789	R	H	E
New York Mets	301	003	020	9	14	2
Los Angeles Dodgers	000	230	000	5	16	2

City's Now Theirs

METS SWEEP DODGERS, ADVANCE TO NLCS BY MIKE VACCARO

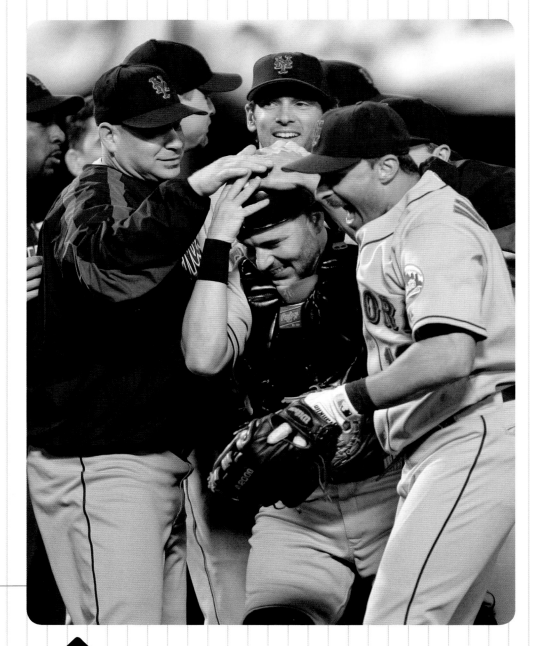

On one coast, a baseball drifted lazily through the smoggy night air, a speck of white framed by a black California sky. It was 8:56 PM, Pacific Time, and as the ball tumbled toward Shawn Green's glove, the ground instantly shifted on another coast, 3,000 miles away, where it was 11:56 PM. and quite suddenly the landscape looked completely different.

New York City, quite suddenly, quite officially, was a Mets town again.

"I can't think of a better day," a soaked, sopping Omar Minaya hoarsely declared through the sticky mist of champagne and revelry, "for our fans."

Surely, neither could those fans. Much of the afternoon had been spent watching the Yankees' uncomfortable death rattle, a season dying in the mirth of Motown. In those precincts of the city dominated by pinstripes and perennial expectation, the day was spent mourning the passage of a most unsatisfying baseball season.

But in those other wards, where orange and blue are the official colors, where "Meet the Mets" is the official hymn, seeing the Yankees lose was merely a warmup. Too many Octobers across the last 20 years have been spent relishing Yankees miseries rather than rooting for Mets successes. Watching the other guys fail grows a little old after a while. Watching your guys succeed is always the better path.

But when you can get a little bit of both on the same day?

"Hey!" Jose Valentin crowed in the middle of the cramped visiting clubhouse at Dodger Stadium, maybe 20 minutes after Green squeezed Ramon Hernandez's can of corn, ending this 9-5 Mets victory and this three-game whitewash of a National League Division Series. "WHO'S THE BEST TEAM IN NEW YORK?"

For the first time since Wednesday, Oct. 12, 1988, the night the Dodgers clipped the Mets in Game 7 of that season's National League Championship Series, there was only one answer to that question, the Mets officially extending a baseball season longer than the Yankees. For the first time in 18 years, they have the most

Mets catcher Paul Lo Duca (center) is congratulated by teammates after the Mets finished off a three-game sweep of the Los Angeles Dodgers to advance to the National League Championship Series. (AP Images)

Michael Tucker slides home ahead of the tag from the Dodgers' Russell Martin in the sixth inning to give the Mets a 6–5 lead. (Getty Images)

meaningful portion of the baseball calendar all to themselves, dancing alone on New York's vast autumnal stage.

A year ago, when Minaya first took control of the franchise's fortunes, when he handed the keys to Willie Randolph and started fattening both the team's bottom line and its winning percentage, the phrase Carlos Beltran coined on the day he signed became the team's official motto: the New Mets.

Now, they can use another one. Because their hometown, for now, for the foreseeable future, and for as long as they keep playing, gets a new name, too.

New Mets City.

Not everyone wanted to concede that the Yankees were loitering invisibly in the clubhouse. Billy Wagner insisted, "We have too much that we want to do for us to worry about what the Yankees are doing or not doing."

But the Yankees were there, make no mistake. The Yankees have shadowed every Mets failure, every shortcoming, every false start, and every dreadful transaction for the better part of those 18 years.

When you share a city and a sport, when you vie for the affections of 7½ million baseball fans every year, you cannot avoid each other. That was

> ## "I can't think of a better day for our fans."
> ### —Omar Minaya, Mets general manager

certainly true across all those Octobers when the Yankees were still standing long after the Mets had gone home.

And so it remains true this time around. For this one day, at least, the Mets hadn't just won the Division Series. They'd won the city back, too.

How long will that last? Only the Mets can determine that much. Starting Wednesday, they get either the Padres or the Cardinals, and they'll be overwhelming favorites to beat either team soundly, as they did during the regular season. After that? Let's be very honest: with the Yankees out of the way, there isn't a team left in the tournament that should frighten the Mets, even with their patchwork pitching rotation, even with Cliff Floyd's continuing tough luck physically.

If they ever should go the distance, yesterday's Yankees loss and last night's Mets victory could turn out to be as watershed a moment in baseball time as any we've ever had in New York City.

Um…make that New Mets City.

	1 2 3	4 5 6	7 8 9	R	H	E
New York Mets	0 1 0	0 2 2	0 2 1	8	16	0
Chicago Cubs	0 0 0	0 0 1	2 0 0	3	9	0

Steady Tom Takes Care of Business

GLAVINE CAPTURES 300TH CAREER WIN BY MIKE VACCARO

The worst part was the seventh inning, of course, because whatever control Chris Glavine felt she held on fate, however peripheral that might have been, it was all gone.

Her husband, Tom, finally had called it a night after 6⅓ innings and 102 pitches in an outdoor steamroom known as Wrigley Field. He had a 5–1 lead. He left a man on second base. He needed eight outs from his bullpen, five days after he'd asked them for the same favor and they'd only been able to get him three.

"I heard from people all night who said I looked like I was about to have a nervous breakdown," Chris Glavine said. "And I was like, 'Well, jeez, what do you expect?' I mean, it's one thing to be Tom, on the field, the ball in your hand, feeling like you have some control over what you're doing. Me? All I can do is wiggle and hop around and wince."

She laughed.

"Then he was out of the game," she said, "and I guess he started to know a little bit about what it's like to be on our side of these games."

The last thing Glavine wanted was to turn this quest for 300 games into a vigil, into the kind of somber parade Alex Rodriguez found himself in the middle of as he tried to hit his 500th home run. That would have been so unlike who Glavine is, and what he's been, across a most extraordinary career. He was the steady one, the consistent one, no flash, no dash, just business.

"I want to go about my business," he would say. "Quietly."

For 6⅓ innings, he'd done his best to keep Wrigley Field as quiet as a requiem mass, but now there were 41,599 people on their feet, lifting their voices to the night sky. A few thousand of them were Mets fans, but they were outnumbered now. The Cubs are in a pennant race. They sensed the Mets' soft underbelly was now melting in the sun.

They scored a run. 5–2.

They scored another run. 5–3.

A young fan holds up a sign as Tom Glavine leaves the dugout during his 300th career win on August 5, 2007, at Wrigley Field in Chicago. Glavine limited the Cubs to two runs in 6⅓ innings. (Getty Images)

Tom Glavine is all smiles at a news conference after earning his 300th career win. A longtime star with the Atlanta Braves, Glavine pitched for the Mets from 2003 through 2007. (AP Images)

Suddenly, in her box seat, Chris Glavine looked like she'd gotten hold of some bad calamari.

"Suddenly," she would say, "I was a little sick to my stomach."

"Suddenly," her husband would admit, "you find yourself saying to yourself, 'Oh no, here we go again.'"

Guillermo Mota gave way to Pedro Feliciano, and Feliciano gave way to Aaron Heilman. Now the tying run was at the plate, and Glavine had crossed his legs in the dugout, and his family members had crossed their fingers and crossed their toes (and maybe crossed themselves, too, for a little added protection), and Heilman delivered, and Ryan Theriot swung.

For a moment, long enough for 41,599 people to emit a loud gasp, long enough for 30 members of the Glavine traveling party to crane their necks and pray, it looked like Theriot may have given the baseball a ride. Maybe earlier in the day, when the wind was blowing straight out, straight onto Lake Michigan, this would have been a galling new plot twist.

Not now. The ball died in the air, then died in Lastings Milledge's mitt. The Mets started adding runs. Billy Wagner, Glavine's carpool partner for home games, was ready to throw the ball 130 miles an hour if necessary. It was all over and the Mets won, 8–3. It was all good.

"Relief," Chris Glavine said. "At last."

There came a moment last night, after the sixth inning, when Glavine walked from the mound and a huge cheer swept across Wrigley, since Kerry Wood was entering a ballgame for the Cubs for the first time in 13 months.

Even when he was a kid on the make with the Braves, Tom Glavine's arm speed was always closer to Wilbur Wood's than Kerry Wood's. He never made scouts weep. He only had that effect on hitters. And last night, he reminded everyone, even those who screamed themselves hoarse welcoming Wood back to the North Side, that stinging your catcher's hand is a fun trait.

But learning how to win is even more fun. Last night, in front of everyone who matters to him, he proved for the 300th time just how much.

"Next time we're all together like this," Chris Glavine said, "it'll be in Cooperstown."

> "Next time we're all together like this, it'll be in Cooperstown."
>
> –Chris Glavine

	123	456	789	R	H	E
New York Mets	102	035	040	15	14	3
New York Yankees	103	001	001	6	12	0

Amazin' Afternoon

DELGADO'S 9 RBIs BURY YANKS IN OPENER BY GEORGE A. KING III

In the middle of a Subway Series game that appeared to be played on quaaludes, Carlos Delgado pumped a river of blue and orange adrenaline into a muggy Bronx afternoon with a record-setting performance in Game 1 of yesterday's day-night, two-ballpark doubleheader.

If ever a game cried for a jolt, the Mets' 15–6 spanking of the Yankees in front of 54,978 at Yankee Stadium was it.

The Yankees looked like a team that arrived home from Pittsburgh a dozen hours before Dan Giese's first pitch. The Mets, who were idle Thursday, didn't show much more life in the early innings.

Enter Delgado, who, with Willie Randolph deleted, has become the main target of Met fans' disgust. All he did was hit a game-busting grand slam in the sixth that almost collided with the back wall in the right-field bleachers, crushed a three-run homer in the eighth, and had a two-run double in the fifth to set a Mets record of nine RBIs.

The previous mark was eight, set by Dave Kingman 32 years ago. Delgado's 12th career slam was the 443rd career blast and moved him past Kingman into 34th place on the all-time list.

"What can I tell you? I came in here pretty pumped up about this series and had a good game. I got lucky," said Delgado, who opened the day hitting .229 with 11 homers, 35 RBIs, and .195 with runners in scoring position. "Every time I came up, it seemed like we had a lot of men on base. I got some good pitches and was able to drive them."

Delgado and the Mets returned to earth in the nightcap at Shea Stadium where Sidney Ponson and some clutch hitting by Bobby Abreu helped the Yankees to a 9-0 victory that was witnessed by 56,308.

Yankee manager Joe Girardi believed his club had a chance to win the first game until Delgado spanked a 3-1 pitch from Ross Ohlendorf.

Carlos Delgado watches one of his two home runs leave the yard. Delgado's nine RBIs set a team record. (AP Images)

Carlos Delgado accepts congratulations from teammate David Wright after Delgado's grand slam in the sixth inning. Delgado also hit a three-run homer in the eighth and knocked in two more runs on a fifth-inning double to finish with nine RBIs. (AP Images)

"I felt if we held them we had a chance to come back, but Delgado killed us today," Girardi said following his club's fourth loss in six games thanks to awful pitching from four chuckers.

The Mets won all three Subway Series games played at Yankee Stadium this year.

Starters Mike Pelfrey and Giese were awful but Pelfrey pilfered a win because his mates battered Giese, Edwar Ramirez, and Ohlendorf. By the time La Troy Hawkins gave up Delgado's three-run homer in the eighth, the result was long decided.

In five innings Pelfrey gave up four runs, eight hits, and walked four. He is 5–6 and on a three-game winning streak.

Giese, who was delayed at Pittsburgh's airport Thursday night, should have stayed away. And gotten rooms for Ramirez and Ohlendorf, who was sent to Triple-A Scranton/Wilkes-Barre after allowing six runs and five hits in 1⅓ innings and watching his ERA balloon to 6.53.

"I got myself in bad counts and didn't throw my slider for strikes," Ohlendorf said. "I had one pitch, a fastball, that's all."

> "What can I tell you? I came in here pretty pumped up about this series and had a good game. I got lucky."
>
> **–Carlos Delgado**

Voices of the Mets

Mets broadcasters Ralph Kiner (left) and Bob Murphy get together before the Mets' 2002 home opener. Kiner and Murphy called Mets games for 42 seasons, from the team's first game in 1962 through Murphy's retirement in 2003. (AP Images)

A fan's closest relationship to his favorite team often comes through seeing and hearing broadcasts of games on television and radio. Over the team's first half century, the Mets' broadcast teams have provided knowledgeable and entertaining commentary and play-by-play descriptions. And unlike many other teams, the Mets broadcasters have remained with the team for lengthy tenures.

The Mets' original broadcast team consisted of Lindsey Nelson, Ralph Kiner, and Bob Murphy. Nelson was one of the best-known broadcasters of his era, known as much for his work calling Notre Dame and NFL football broadcasts as for his work in baseball. Murphy honed his broadcasting skills calling Boston Red Sox and Baltimore Orioles games from 1954 to 1961. Kiner was a Hall of Fame slugger for the Pittsburgh Pirates in the 1940s and 1950s, chasing Babe Ruth's single-season home run record and slugging 369 home runs before a back injury forced him to retire at age 32. Nelson, Kiner, and Murphy shared both television and radio duties using a rotational system from 1962 to 1979. The radio booth was manned by one announcer at all times, while the television side was manned by one or two announcers, changing throughout the game. Often, one announcer would take a two- or

Also known for his work on national football broadcasts, Lindsey Nelson teamed with Ralph Kiner and Bob Murphy to call Mets games on radio and television from 1962 to 1978. (AP Images)

A young Bob Murphy is shown in the Polo Grounds press box in 1963. Murphy called Mets games for 42 seasons. (AP Images)

three-inning break. The Mets did not begin employing two or more announcers in the booth until the 1980s.

Nelson left the Mets after the 1978 season and was replaced in the rotation by Steve Albert. Beginning in 1982, the Mets switched to having separate radio teams on television and radio. Murphy took on radio duties, sharing the booth with various announcers over the next 22 seasons. Kiner became part of the television broadcast team. Former major league catcher Tim McCarver shared the Mets television booth with Kiner from 1983 to 1998. Former Mets stars Bud Harrelson and Rusty Staub were also part of the Mets' television team in the 1980s.

Gary Cohen was barely 30 years old when he joined Bob Murphy in the Mets' radio booth for the 1989 season. Known for his signature phrases and vivid game descriptions, Cohen took over as the Mets' lead radio voice following Murphy's retirement in 2003. In 2006, he moved to the television booth where he joined Keith Hernandez and Ron Darling. Hernandez, the star first baseman for the 1980s Mets teams, began broadcasting Mets games in 1999. Other than his Gold Glove play at first base and knowledgeable insight, Hernandez is also known for his appearances on the television show *Seinfeld*. Darling won 136 games over 13 big-league seasons and went 15–6 for the 1986 World Series champion Mets. He began his broadcasting career with the Washington Nationals in 2005 and joined the Mets the following season. The television team of Cohen, Hernandez, and Darling remains in place. Now in his late eighties, Kiner continues to participate in Mets broadcasts on a part-time basis.

Mets great Tom Seaver also called televised games for the Mets in the early 2000s, teaming with veteran broadcaster Gary Thorne. Seaver was known for his expert insight into pitching situations.

Howie Rose has been uttering his catch phrase "Put it in the books" following Mets victories since 1995. Rose moved back and forth from the radio booth to the cable television booth from 1995 to 2005. In 2006, after Cohen moved to the television booth, Rose took over as the Mets' lead radio voice.

Ralph Kiner takes notes during a game at Shea Stadium in 1985. A Hall of Fame slugger and part of the Mets' original broadcast team, Kiner was still participating in Mets broadcasts on a part-time basis in 2011. (AP Images)

Tim McCarver, a former star catcher himself, interviews Mets backstop Gary Carter. McCarver was the television voice of the Mets from 1983 to 1998. (Getty Images)

Ron Darling waves to the crowd before throwing out the first pitch before Game 7 of the 2006 National League Championship Series. Darling won 99 games for the Mets between 1983 and 1991 and has been part of the Mets' broadcast team since 2006. (AP Images)

Keith Hernandez and Bud Harrelson share a few words in 2002. Both men were All-Star players for the Mets who later worked in the Mets' broadcast booth. (Spencer A. Burnett/New York Post)

Mets broadcasters (from left) Gary Cohen, Ron Darling, and Keith Hernandez share the booth with 10-year-old Kyle Singh. Singh won the privilege of calling a half-inning by winning SNY's "Kidscaster Contest" with an essay about Carlos Delgado. (Getty Images)

Gary Cohen smiles in the Shea Stadium radio booth before a 2002 game. Cohen has called Mets games since 1989. In 2006, he moved from the radio booth to the television booth. (Charles Wenzelberg/New York Post)

Mookie Wilson points to the famous ball that went between Bill Buckner's legs during Game 6 of the 1986 World Series. The ball is on display at the Mets museum at Citi Field. (Charles Wenzelberg/New York Post)